Lost Gold and Silver Mines of the Southwest

EUGENE L. CONROTTO

MAPS BY
NORTON ALLEN

DOVER PUBLICATIONS, INC.
Mineola, New York

ACKNOWLEDGMENTS

To the past and present publishers of Desert Magazine for their assistance and cooperation.

To Asa M. Russell for permission to reprint the entire text of his Sept., 1955, Desert Magazine article.

To Charles W. Polzer, S. J., for permission to quote large passages of his August, 1962, Desert Magazine article.

Copyright

Published in Canada by General Publishing Company, Ltd., 30 Lesmill Road, Don Mills, Toronto, Ontario.

Published in the United Kingdom by Constable and Company, Ltd., 3 The Lanchesters, 162–164 Fulham Palace Road, London W6 9ER.

Bibliographical Note

This Dover edition, first published in 1996, is an unabridged republication of the work originally published by Best-West Publications / Desert-Southwest Publishers, Palm Desert, California, in 1963 under the title *Lost Desert Bonanzas*.

Library of Congress Cataloging-in-Publication Data

Conrotto, Eugene L.

Lost gold and silver mines of the Southwest / Eugene L. Conrotto ; maps by Norton Allen.

p.   cm.

Originally published: Lost desert bonanzas. Palm Desert, Calif. : Best-West Publications, 1963.

Includes bibliographical references and index.

ISBN 0-486-29275-4 (pbk.)

1. Treasure-trove—Southwest, New. 2. Treasure-trove—Mexico—Sonora (State) 3. Treasure-trove—Mexico—Baja California. 4. Gold mines and mining—Southwest, New—History. 5. Silver mines and mining—Southwest, New—History. 6. Southwest, New—History, Local. 7. Gold mines and mining—Mexico—Sonora (State)—History. 8. Silver mines and mining—Mexico—Sonora (State)—History. 9. Gold mines and mines and mining—Mexico—Baja California—History. 10. Silver mines and mining—Mexico—Baja California—History. I. Title.

F786.C66   1996

979—dc20   96-20462

                                                                              CIP

Manufactured in the United States of America
Dover Publications, Inc., 31 East 2nd Street, Mineola, N.Y. 11501

FOR JEANNE AND DUANE
TREASURE FOUND

Foreword

ABOUT ONCE A MONTH, into the offices of Desert Magazine come men with a purpose. They usually travel in pairs or in threes, driving a pickup truck or four-wheel-drive rig. Their clothes are clean and serviceable: sun-faded jeans, plaid shirt, hiking boots. They themselves are clean-shaven, and they are obviously well-educated, speaking English and not the mutilated twang of the stereotyped "old prospector" of the D movie.

These men are tanned and hardened—accustomed to the outdoors and its demands; but their livelihoods are earned in a big city. Their idea of a good time is to spend a week or a month as far away from the paved roads as possible—and they are the kind of men who can get in (and out) of the most rugged country. With a foot of baling wire and a ton of self-reliance, they can fix any vehicle that burns gasoline.

They are as familiar with backcountry springs and trails as the average person is with the main roads of his hometown. They know and appreciate the history of the Southwest. They are acquainted with the literature of the desert country and know its artists and naturalists. They are particularly savvy about geology and mineralogy.

But, so help me, they are crazy!

Crazy because they have let one slim rumor or one set of circumstances or one chance meeting on the trail with a person possessed come to rule their lives. They are Lost Mine Hunters, specializing in one mine (at a time), and owning (they are convinced) more of its puzzle-pieces than anyone else.

They always start their conversation with: "Some years ago, *DESERT* ran a story on a . . . " Always looking for one more piece of the puzzle!

After we locate the back copy of the magazine that contains the story or some mention of a lost mine, our guests open up a little and tell about their search to date (omitting a few of the more important clues, of course). And when they are about to leave, I find myself—always—saying good-bye with these words: "Good luck—and if you find the mine (or treasure), be sure you write a story on the discovery for *DESERT* . . . "

So far, the magazine has not printed such an article.

During the past 25 years, the lost mines and treasure we have described in the magazine remain lost. Some of the stories were about the legendary El Dorados; others were original, told for the first time by the men who actually found—and then lost—their one chance on earth to live on Easy Street.

This book is a condensation of those articles, reprinting where possible the maps which appeared with the original article. In a few instances where the *DESERT* story did not have a map (or the map was amateurish), new maps were drawn for this book.

All maps—except Kino's chart on page 221—are by Norton Allen, whose name is synonymous with desertland cartography. Nothing said here can add to the worth of these maps. They speak for themselves. Individually and collectively they offer a banquet to those who would travel in body or spirit to the remote corners of the lonely, lovely desert land.

In writing these synopses, I have tried to place emphasis on the known "facts" concerning each lost bonanza—the very information which the serious searcher would glean from the original magazine article.

In getting to the meat of the stories in the old issues of *DESERT*, color and romance have been sacrificed. Those readers who want the "full treatment" on any or all of the episodes contained in this book, can learn the availability and prices of particular *DESERT* back issues by writing to the Magazine at Palm Desert, Calif. (Month and year of each *DESERT* from which the chapters of this book were condensed are given in the text.)

A final word: if all the clues to a lost mine were known, the bonanza would not be lost. An honest effort has been made here to detail all known puzzle-pieces. The rest is up to you. Good luck—and if you find the mine (or treasure), be sure you write a story on the discovery for *DESERT* . . .

There's always a first time.

—ELC
Autumn, 1963

CONTENTS

The Lost Bonanzas:

* * *

APPENDIX:

The Pearl Ship

THE SALTON SEA, created in the early years of this century by a break in the Colorado River, is not the first body of water to fill the below-sea-level trough of the Colorado Desert. Geologists know that several invasions by Colorado River waters have occurred over the centuries.

The most recent of these lost seas was Lake Cahuilla. It may have existed in post-Columbian times, which means that the white man and Lake Cahuilla were in this hemisphere at the same time. And the white man extended his new world mainly by ship.

In 1615, Juan DeIturbe, after a successful season of pearl fishing and bartering with the Indians along the coast of the Gulf of California, sailed north seeking the Straits of Anian—fabled water route to the Atlantic.

The head of the Gulf narrowed into a channel between two mountain ranges. DeIturbe sailed on, and soon his ship entered a large body of water.

The Spanish ship did not leave this inland sea. A flashflood roaring out of the mountains, blocked the channel. After several weeks of futile search for an exit from the inland sea, the ship and most of its pearl treasure was abandoned.

One hundred and sixty years later, a young muleteer in the DeAnza expedition stumbled upon the ship two or three days out of Yuma. He filled his pockets with pearls and deserted westward to the Pacific and the mission at San Diego. Later, he returned to the mountains, befriended some Indians, and in their company made several searches of the Colorado Desert for his rotting ship—in vain.

This is one version of the Lost Ship in the Salton Basin. There are two others.

In 1862, a Los Angeles man named Joshua Talbot was one of a small party of gold seekers bound for the mines of LaPaz, Arizona.

The outfit ordered a 21-foot skiff built in Los Angeles. Records show that such a craft was turned out in the workshop of Perry & Woodworth late in May, 1862.

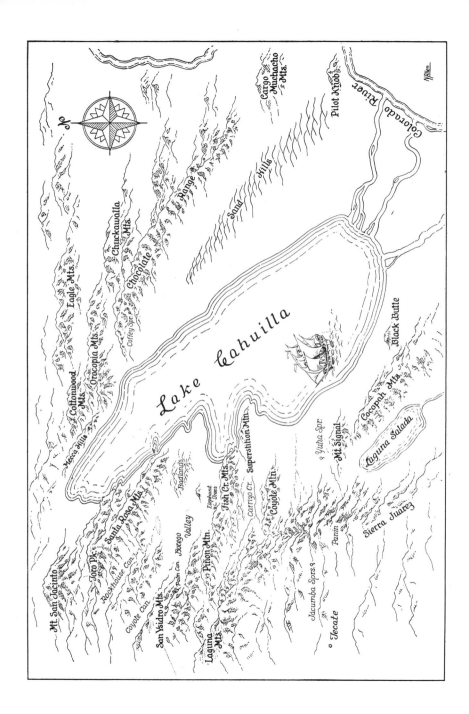

The *LOS ANGELES STAR* for May 31, 1862, had this to say about Talbot's boat: "It was built for one of the companies starting for the mines, to be used in crossing the river. The Colorado now is greatly swollen from the heavy rains in the mountains, and there is no ferry established at the mines: it is a provident forethought to go prepared to cross the stream without loss of time or obstruction."

The boat was put on wheels and the journey across the desert undertaken. But June is no time to tackle the Low Desert. The teams gave out and Talbot and his companions were forced to abandon ship. No doubt they made some effort to conceal the valuable craft, but there is nothing in the record to indicate that they returned to salvage it. In less than a decade, the Talbot boat was a legend. In 1870 Indians reported having seen the craft.

Its location was given as 40 miles north of the San Bernardino-Yuma Road, and about 30 miles west of Dos Palmas.

That same year (1870), a party headed by Charles Clusker made a try for the boat. Local newspapers reported that the Clusker party found it 50 miles or more from Dos Palmas "in a region of boiling mud springs." The men returned to civilization to secure equipment for "reaching the boat." Here the record fades completely.

Version Number Three introduces no new ship, but gives substantial modern-day confirmation of the fact that some sort of ship does exist in the Salton Desert. The story was told in the January, 1939, *DESERT* by Charles C. Niehuis, who interviewed and photographed the principal involved, Perta Socia Tucker, at the time she was visiting her second husband, Jim, at the Arizona Pioneers' Home in Prescott.

Perta's first husband, Santiago Socia, is the one who knew of the ship's location: "a narrow box canyon with high sheer walls, and a sandy bottom; and partially buried there, a boat of ancient appearance—an open boat but big, with round metal disks on its sides."

The Socias lived in Tecate, Baja California. "One time," Perta told reporter Niehuis, "my husband, Santiago, was riding in the mountains in

The old Liverpool Salt Works near Indio. This plant was inundated in the 1905-06 flood which created Salton Sea.

the *Estados,* and I was with him. We was up high, and could see more mountains, 15, maybe 20 miles away, and he stop and say: 'Perta, I am a poor man, now, and maybe some time I die before you, and leave nothing.

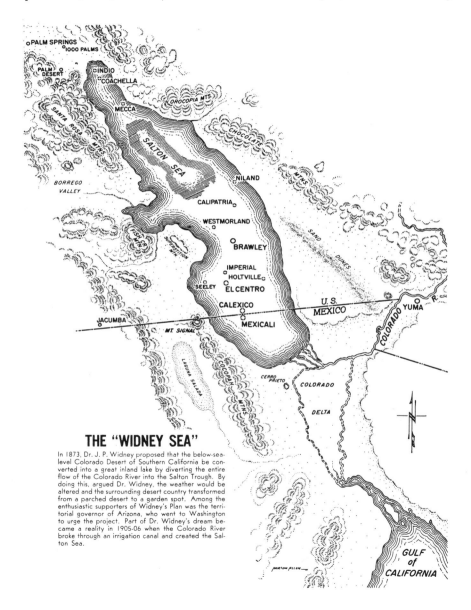

THE "WIDNEY SEA"

In 1873, Dr. J. P. Widney proposed that the below-sea-level Colorado Desert of Southern California be converted into a great inland lake by diverting the entire flow of the Colorado River into the Salton Trough. By doing this, argued Dr. Widney, the weather would be altered and the surrounding desert country transformed from a parched desert to a garden spot. Among the enthusiastic supporters of Widney's Plan was the territorial governor of Arizona, who went to Washington to urge the project. Part of Dr. Widney's dream became a reality in 1905-06 when the Colorado River broke through an irrigation canal and created the Salton Sea.

You get a good man, and come back here. You go to those mountains,' and he point, 'the ship, it is there'."

Today, thousands of boats play on the waters of the Salton Sea. Did another, earlier, vessel sail into this trough? The only fact present here is that the legend of a Lost Ship in the Desert is a long lived one. It has been woven by three tongues: Spanish, Indian and English.

THE FLOOD OF '91

In 1891 when Southern Pacific trainmen reported the sudden appearance of a mysterious "lake" in the great desert basin west of the Algodones Dunes, the people of Yuma became alarmed lest the rising waters cut-off their rail lifeline with the coast. While in actuality the water spreading over the Alamo River drainage was a seasonal overflow from the west bank of the Colorado River, some Yuma residents feared the water was from rising tides of the Gulf of California. Explorer Godfrey Sykes and a companion volunteered to trace the flood's origin. Did a Spanish pearl ship follow this same course in a similar, earlier flood?

Underground River

In the March, 1940, *DESERT*, readers were given the John D. Mitchell version of a persistent Mojave Desert lost treasure tale.

The basics are these: the gold is scattered in black sand; the black sand lies deep under the ground along a subterranean lake or river; the supply of gold-bearing sand is endless.

Mitchell's gold is discovered by two Paiute Indians "high up along the eastern edge of Death Valley and not many hours' journey from Scotty's Castle." The Paiutes were trudging along "over the hot sands on the western edge of a dry lake" when they spied the caved-in mouth of a tunnel. Investigating, they found a large underground pool and, of course, the gold-flecked black sand.

While attempting to swim to an island in the center of the pool, one of the Indians drowned. His brother, honoring a taboo against frequenting a place where death has entered, left the cave and never returned.

In the May, 1961, *DESERT*, Paul F. Patchick briefly outlined the more popular version of this story. The locale shifts southward from Death Valley to "haunted" Crystal Cave on the northern flank of Kokoweef Peak in the Ivanpah Mountains.

The Southwest mining fraternity was set astir in the 1920s when a miner named E. P. Dorr swore in an affidavit that he had discovered a swiftly flowing river deep under Kokoweef Peak; and lining its banks were sands rich in gold.

There's nothing unreal about Crystal Cave. It exists, but it is believed Dorr damaged it beyond use with dynamite. In any event, it is private property and at last report the Crystal Cave Mining Corporation wants nothing to do with lost gold or lost river hunters. Two cave explorers lost their lives here in 1959.

John Mitchell comes back in the August, 1951, *DESERT*, with a somewhat similar yarn. This one involves an old prospector who told his story to Mitchell around the turn of the century. The old man had picked-up four pounds of gold nuggets "in a black sand deposit near the Clark Mountains northeast of Nippeno (now called Nipton)." The cave of the black sands was "on the east side of a small limestone hill about 50 feet above the level of the dry lake bed."

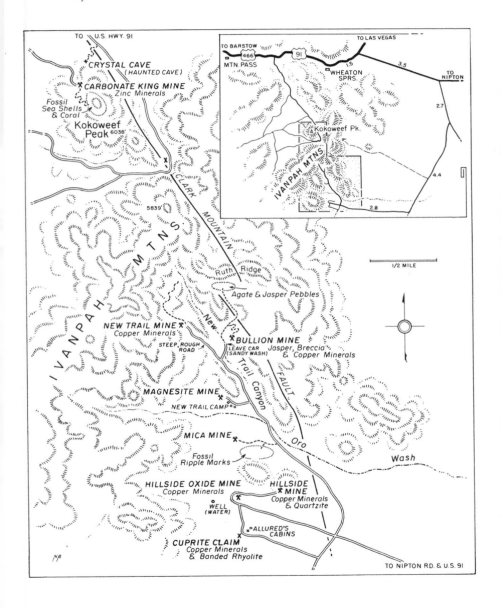

Apache Gold Mine

JOHN D. MITCHELL writes in the April, 1940, *DESERT*, that "according to rumor" the rich vein in question was first discovered by Apache Indians (who had about as much use for gold "in the latter part of the 18th Century" as they did for the other diseases the white man brought into this country).

A half-dozen Spanish soldiers, in a detail bound for Zuni, were ordered to stay behind and work the rich vein. It was located "somewhere in the wild and picturesque Verde River country, not far from Jerome." To be more specific, and quoting a source from "Mexico," Mitchell places the mine in the "Sycamore Canyon country between Jerome and Perkinsville, Yavapai County . . . there are numerous small side canyons that empty their flood waters into the Sycamore and at least one of them answers the description . . ."

After the six had gathered all the gold their animals could carry, they beat a retreat from the canyon. But, the Apaches caught them and four of the Spaniards were butchered. "Ten days later the two (survivors) arrived at Tubac on the Santa Cruz River."

It was 1767—the year of the Jesuit Expulsion from the New World. The frontier withered after the Jesuits were banished, and consequently the mine was never again visited by a white man.

As a further clue, Mitchell offers the information that "the old map shows the profile of an Indian's head sculptured by nature on a high cliff just above the mine opening. The nose of this rock Indian is very large and as the story goes the mine is located directly under the Indian's nose. It is said there is such a cliff overlooking a narrow box canyon up in that part of the country and the foundations of an old adobe or rock house are still visible. The rock fence or wall at the foot of the high cliff which was known to many old time cowmen who ranged their cattle in that part of the country, is now almost completely covered by a slide of rock from the canyon wall above. A stream of water breaks under a large boulder near the canyon wall and the ruins of an old adobe smelter and the grinding stones of an arrastre may still be seen there. Not far away under the trees are several old graves all marked by piles of stone."

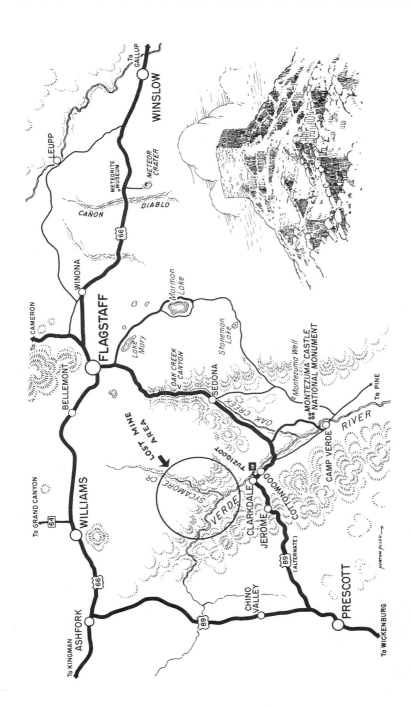

Lost Pick Mine

BRONCO CANYON is 50 miles north of Phoenix; 25 miles northwest of Fort McDowell. In 1871 it was habitated by an Apache Indian who never seemed to lack for gold.

One day two prospectors, Brown and Davis, followed the Apache home from a store in Phoenix. Later, on the west side of Bronco, the two Anglos found "an 18-inch quartz vein very rich in free gold similar in form to that they had seen in the hands of the Indian."

Brown and Davis built an arrastre at a nearby spring and milled 25 sacks of quartz — $80,000. But a band of Apaches attacked and Davis was killed instantly. Brown crawled into a thicket and escaped.

At age 80 he returned to Arizona and made preparations for a jaunt into Bronco Canyon. He fell ill, and told his story on his deathbed.

The balls of amalgam in which the $80,000 in gold was collected were buried in a "shallow hole between a large boulder and a stratum of white volcanic ash that outcrops along the foot of the mountains on the east side of the little valley."

The pick? Brown said his partner's pick was in the face of the quartz vein. Years later a Mexican goatherder brought a story into town: he had seen a rusty pick stuck in a quartz outcrop, but had not stopped to investigate.

The story is in the May, 1940, *DESERT*. Its author is John D. Mitchell.

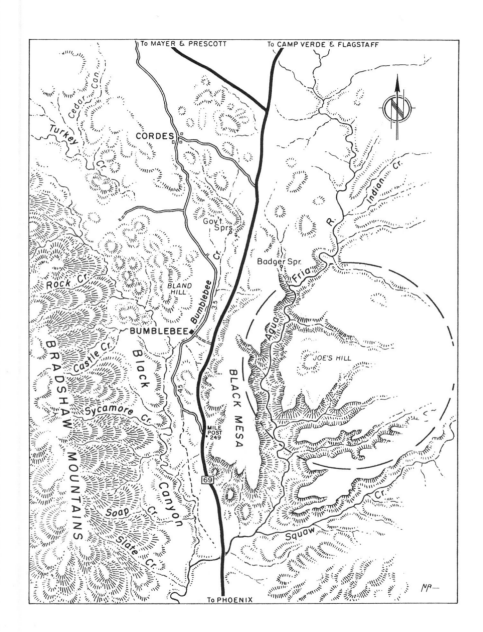

Native Silver Mine

SOUTHERN ARIZONA's Arivaca-Tubac area is silver country, but the specimens found along Carrizo Creek apparently were spectacular enough to create quite a stir.

John Connors, ex-miner, was operating a saloon in Nogales when a prospector came to him with a fist-sized silver nugget. The prospector had bought the specimen for a few dollars from an Opata Indian who found it along the Carrizo while hunting deer.

Connors grubstaked the prospector who spent several months in the field, then returned to Nogales with four burros loaded down with rich ore. He told Connors the silver was plentiful "farther along Carrizo Creek toward the Mexican line."

Naturally the prospector had to celebrate the fact that he was about to become a millionaire. He hit the bottle too hard and died from exposure.

Connors tried to find the silver source, but was not successful.

The story, by John D. Mitchell, is in *DESERT'S* June, 1940, issue.

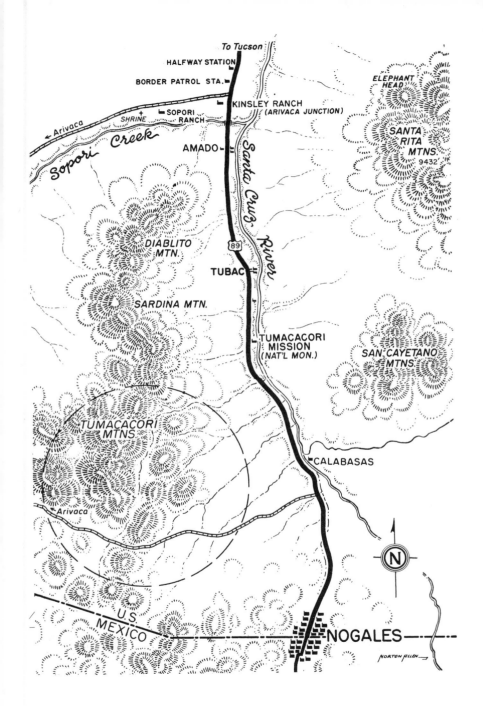

Bullion Black Gold

THIS IS PERHAPS the wildest of all lost mine stories appearing in the pages of *DESERT*. Not too many years ago, an honest man would tell you that the desert had valleys and hills that were "poisonous," that is, people believed there were some areas of the desert in which poison vapors made human existence impossible.

In John D. Mitchell's "Black Gold" (August, 1940, *DESERT*), such a place is described (Uncle Sam should be warned that it is dangerously close to the Twentynine Palms Marine Corps Base). It's in the Bullion Mountain country "on the desert between Bagdad (California, that is) and Twentynine Palms." The black gold (related to "Pegleg" Smith's treasure — although the Pegleg in Mitchell's story is likely not the same man) lay "in the center of one of the many dry lakes known to exist there." The gold outcrop, to be more specific, is in the form of a chimney reposing on a "small black mountain" standing in turn, on the above-mentioned dry lake.

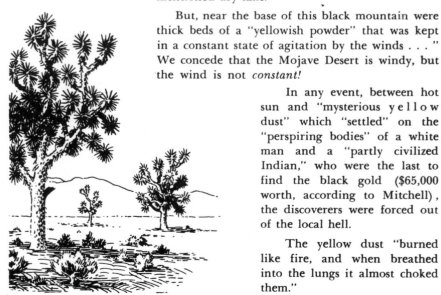

But, near the base of this black mountain were thick beds of a "yellowish powder" that was kept in a constant state of agitation by the winds . . ." We concede that the Mojave Desert is windy, but the wind is not *constant!*

In any event, between hot sun and "mysterious y e l l o w dust" which "settled" on the "perspiring bodies" of a white man and a "partly civilized Indian," who were the last to find the black gold ($65,000 worth, according to Mitchell), the discoverers were forced out of the local hell.

The yellow dust "burned like fire, and when breathed into the lungs it almost choked them."

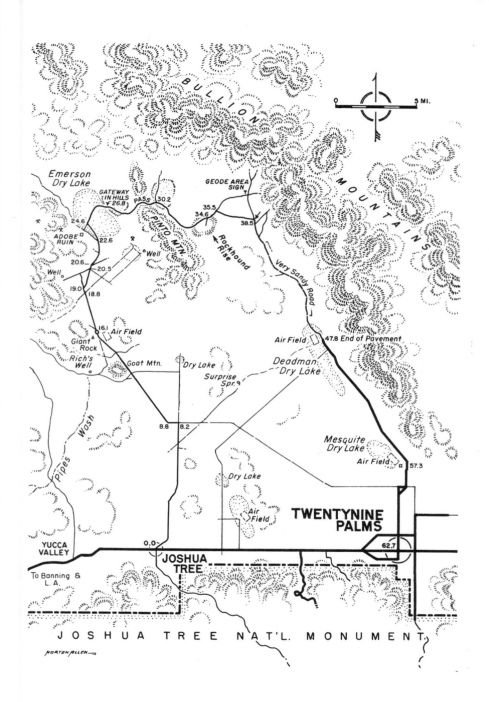

Golden Eagle

In 1902 "Alkali" Jones, prospector, was on a *pasear* from Skidoo, California, to Searchlight, Nevada. In between lay Death Valley.

Two days out of Skidoo, he was caught in a sandstorm, so he groped his way to a small butte and took shelter among the granite boulders at its base.

When the blue sky reappeared, Alkali attempted to regain his bearings. He climbed the butte (the north face). Half-way up he found milky white quartz shot through with gold. The vein was three feet wide.

As Alkali scribbled out a location notice, he looked up and saw a huge bird in the sky. Not pretending to be an ornithologist, he admittedly made a guess and called his mine the "Golden Eagle."

John D. Mitchell (*DESERT*, October, 1940) says Alkali climbed out of the valley onto Coffin Mountain in the Funeral Range. From his perch he surveyed the pink granite butte and its rosy dreams, and pondered his far less rosy fate: he was without water.

He wandered around until he found a pothole full of water. Then he proceeded to Searchlight via Charleston Mountain, Goodsprings and Crescent.

The nine pounds of gold rock he had taken from the butte brought him $180, with which he bought burros and supplies. He went back for more gold—but was never heard from again.

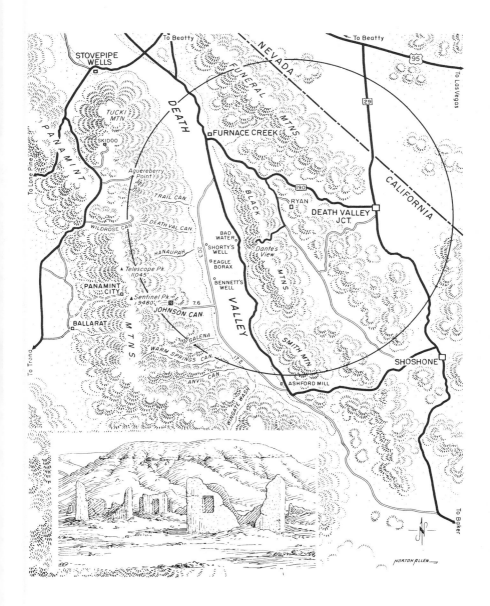

To Beatty

NEVADA

STOVEPIPE WELLS

95

To Las Vegas

To Beatty

TUCKI MTN

FUNERAL

SKIDOO

DEATH

MTNS

29

PANAMINT

To Lone Pine

Aguereberry Point

FURNACE CREEK

TRAIL CAN.

CALIFORNIA

190

BLACK

RYAN

DEATH VALLEY JCT.

DEATH VAL CAN.

WILDROSE CAN.

BAD WATER

SHORTY'S WELL

HANAUPAH

Telescope Pk. 11,045'

EAGLE BORAX

Dantes View

203

BENNETT'S WELL

PANAMINT CITY

Sentinel Pk. 9480'

MTNS

JOHNSON CAN.

VALLEY

7.6

BALLARAT

M T N S

GALENA

WARM SPRINGS CAN.

SMITH MTN.

SHOSHONE

To Trona

17.2

ANVIL CAN.

ASHFORD MILL

WINGATE WASH

To Baker

NORTON ALLEN

Silver of Pish-la-ki

CHARLES KELLY, esteemed Utah historian, brought to the pages of *DESERT* (December, 1940) an interview with a Navajo which bears directly on one of the West's great lost mine tales.

It concerns the silver found by the ill-fated Merrick and Mitchell in Monument Valley—the authenticity of which there can be no doubt.

Merrick and Mitchell were killed in 1880 by a group of Navajos led by Chief Hoskaninni—the "Angry One"—who hid out for five years, during which time (and this, too, is unrefutable) he worked native silver into ornaments.

Historian Kelly was on the trail of facts concerning Cass Hite, hermit of the Colorado River country, when he met and interviewed 82-year-old Hoskaninni-begay, son of the Hoskaninni who had participated in the Merrick-Mitchell killing.

"I asked this old Navajo gentleman to tell me the story of the lost Pish-la-ki Mine and of Hosteen Pish-la-ki (Cass Hite) who came to search for it," wrote Kelly.

This is what Hoskaninni-begay said during that 1939 interview:

". . . I remember those two men who were killed in Monument Valley . . . Always they were looking at the rocks and every day they stopped somewhere to dig. They came in late summer and stayed until after the first snow. At that time my father's camp was on the east side of Navajo Mountain. Not far from our camp I saw the tracks of their horses in snow . . . A few days later we heard they had been killed near what the white men call Mitchell Butte, by the Utes. In those days there were still many Utes in Monument Valley . . .

"Pish-la-ki? I knew him well. He and my father were just like brothers. The first time I saw that man was at our camp below Kayenta, about two years after the prospectors were killed. He walked into camp one day and sat down by the fire. He had made himself our guest according to Navajo custom, so we took care of his horses and gave him a sheepskin to sleep on. He talked to us by signs because he did not understand our lan-

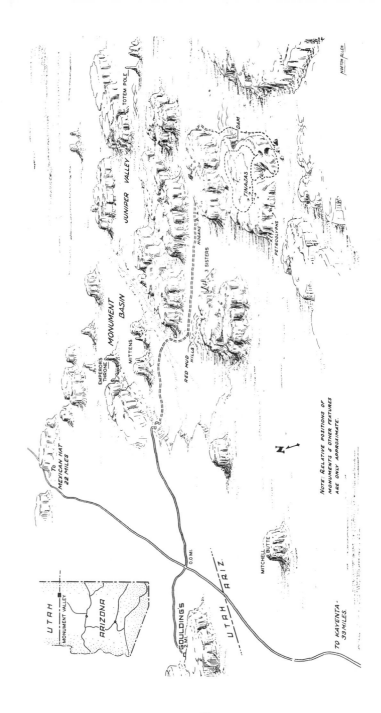

MORTON ALLEN

TOTEM POLE

JUNIPER VALLEY

DAM

TINAJAS

PETROGLYPHS

HOGAN'S

3 SISTERS

MONUMENT BASIN

EMPERORS THRONE

MITTENS

RED MUD HILLS

TO MEXICAN HAT 22 MILES

N

NOTE: RELATIVE POSITIONS OF MONUMENTS & OTHER FEATURES ARE ONLY APPROXIMATE.

MITCHELL BUTTE

0.0 MI.

GOULDINGS 2 MI.

UTAH
ARIZ.

TO KAVENTA 33 MILES.

UTAH

MONUMENT VALLEY

ARIZONA

guage. In his pack he had many kinds of ore. He showed me a piece of heavy black rock and asked me if I had seen anything like it in our country.

". . . nearly all rock here is red; but a few days before, while riding on Skeleton Mesa, I had picked up a small piece of black rock. I showed this to our visitor and when he looked at it through a glass, he nearly fell backward into the fire with surprise . . .

"He stayed with us three months and soon learned to speak our language. We called him Pish-la-ki because he was always looking for silver . . . On Skeleton Mesa we found a small sack full of black rocks. We found green rocks in Copper Canyon, but we never found a silver mine.

"Father and I . . . took Pish-la-ki out to the railroad at Winslow . . . About a year later I was riding in Copper Canyon when I saw the footprints of a white man. Following them I found Pish-la-ki, and we embraced like brothers. He was still hunting for silver. Again we rode together for many days but found nothing . . .

"There was a place where we used to dig silver from the rocks, and hammer it into ornaments. In those days our silver work was plain, not decorated with designs nor set with turquoise like it is now. We got silver from that place whenever we wanted it. But we knew we would be driven out of the country if white men found that mine, so we kept it a secret. Only seven men knew its location. One by one those men grew old and died. When the last one was dying he called his oldest son and tried to tell him how to find the mine. The son searched for many months, but could never find it. Now the secret is lost. My father was one of the seven, but he never allowed me to go there with him.

"I have seen silver that came from that place. Some of it is buried with my father. Pish-la-ki taught me to know silver ore, and I have hunted for that mine for a long time. Now I am old and poor, but still whenever I ride I look at the ground, and think maybe some day I will find that rich mine. Then my children would not be hungry."

The sequel to this story is told by Randall Henderson in the December, 1950, *DESERT*. Harry Goulding of Goulding's Trading Post in Monument Valley, grubstaked a Navajo who knew where the Pish-la-ki silver lay—but was reluctant to go in after it. The Navajo finally agreed to haul out some silver, but he made a botch of the endeavor, losing his string of burros. The gods, he insisted, were displeased.

———————

HENRY CHEE DODGE, venerable leader of the Navajos, added an interesting angle to this business of precious metal on the reservation. He was interviewed for *DESERT* (November, 1938) by Mrs. White Mountain Smith.

In the 1880s the rumors were persistent: there was gold and silver in Navajoland. In fact, a Navajo named Osh-ka-ni-ne had shown some rich specimens around the trading posts. Quite a few prospectors followed the leads supplied to them by Osh-ka-ni-ne, and quite a few prospectors were never seen again.

"When a miner disappeared," Dodge revealed, "his horses and goods found their way to the hogan of Osh-ka-ni-ne."

The outlaw and his accomplices were arrested by Dodge, but they did not swing for their crimes. After all, reasoned the law, the white miners were in Navajoland to steal from the Indians.

Adams Diggings

THIS JOHN D. MITCHELL yarn (July, 1941, *DESERT*) has a solid historical base. We quote Lieutenant W. H. Emory (*Notes of a Military Reconnaissance From Fort Leavenworth in Kansas to San Diego in California*—1848) : "The Prieto (Black) River flows down from the mountains freighted with gold. Its sands are said to be full of the precious metal. A few adventurers who ascended the river hunting beaver washed the sands at night when they halted and were richly rewarded. Tempted by their success, they made a second trip and were attacked and most of them killed by the Indians. My authority for this statement is Landreau, who, though an illiterate man, is truthful."

Escaping with Landreau was a man named Adams. They headed south from the scene of the Black River Massacre and were rescued by Army scouts near the headwaters of the Gila River.

Two decades later Adams made a bid to relocate the cabin he and his partners had built on the Black. Under its floorboards was buried $60,000 in gold dust. It was too late.

A LATTER DAY ADAMS who also lost a mine is the subject of a letter in *DESERT'S* May, 1944, issue, written by Thomas Childs of Rowood, Arizona.

From 1883 through the 1920s, Childs made several attempts to trackdown some gold which kept cropping-up in his life. In 1925, a man named Adams brought-in some nuggets which he said had been picked-up "northwest of three peaks two or three miles" from Rowood. "The peaks he mentioned are known by the Indians as Tan Babia, or High Well."

In '83, Childs had seen gold from the same area in the hands of an Indian. Where did the Adams gold come from? ". . . a white quartz ledge that crossed a small wash . . ."

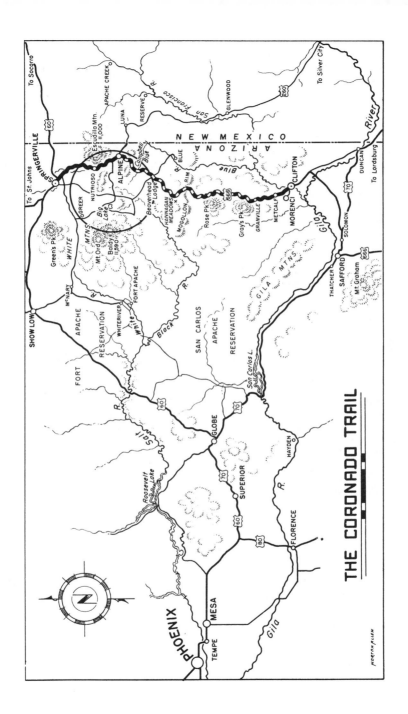

THE CORONADO TRAIL

Dutch Oven Mine

"Tom Schofield's lost mine was supposed to be 10 miles north of Danby in the Clipper Mountains."

If all lost mines were at the point where they were supposed to be, there would be no lost mines. However, since 1894, Mojave Desert chroniclers have been spotting the Lost Dutch Oven Mine in the Clipper Mountains. They all tell about a narrow, rock-walled canyon and other landmarks. "All are highly colored by their authors, this one no more nor less than the rest."

In June, 1894—say all versions of this tale—Thomas Schofield walked into Los Angeles with his pockets filled with gold.

"Young Schofield said he had been drilling a tunnel in the Clipper Mountains in search of a flow of underground water for the Santa Fe Railroad."

One day he took a day off to do a little looking around. He tracked a mountain sheep into a gulch, and there saw an old trail which he decided to follow. It led "to a spring that trickled from a wall of rock to form a pool at its base. Back-tracking over the trail he traced it . . . over three low hills, the hogback of two ranges, and then into another canyon."

The trail pitched up a steep hill. "His curiosity impelled him to go on toward two upright rocks, a cleft in the side of the mountain."

Beyond the cleft Schofield picked-up the trail. It led directly to a black mass of rock, skirted it, and came to an old mining camp.

Above the camp—reached by a narrow, steep trail—was a well-timbered shaft—the gold mine!

Tom had a wonderful afternoon sampling the vein, looking over the old mine tools, dreaming about how life would be as a rich man. By nightfall, however, he was out of the clouds and sorely in need of food and drink—of which the camp only provided the latter.

"Disgustedly, he kicked off the lid of the iron Dutch oven. Instead of food he saw gold!"

This is where the unknown miners had stored their highgrade. But,

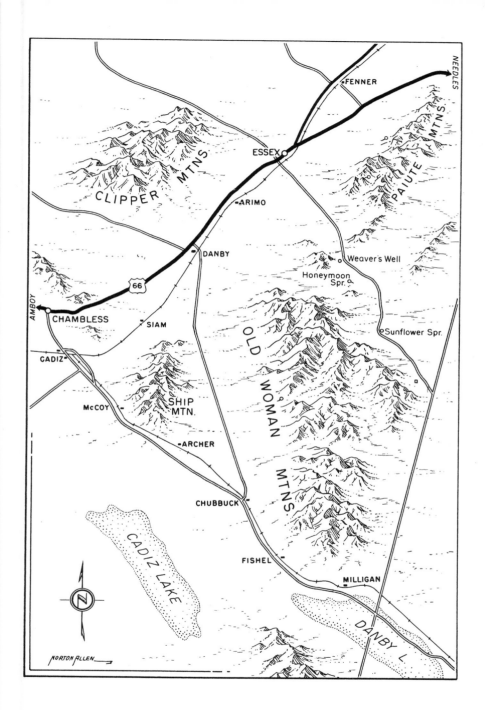

NEEDLES

FENNER

PAIUTE MTNS.

CLIPPER MTNS

ESSEX

ARIMO

DANBY

Weaver's Well

Honeymoon Spr.

66

Sunflower Spr.

AMBOY

CHAMBLESS

SIAM

OLD WOMAN MTNS.

CADIZ

SHIP MTN.

McCOY

ARCHER

CHUBBUCK

CADIZ LAKE

FISHEL

MILLIGAN

N

DANBY L.

NORTON ALLEN

in the long view of things, we must conclude that this was an unlucky discovery for Tom. It was the start of a life of frustration, for he was never able to retrace his steps to the camp after he had departed the scene —and he lived the rest of his many years in the shadow of his bitter bonanza. He was 80 years of age when Rexford Bellamy interviewed him for the October, 1941, *DESERT* story.

There is a Dutch Oven Mine, and it is at the end of a trail exactly as described by Schofield. But, it is in the Old Woman Mountains, 20 miles south of the Clippers. The old man would neither confirm or deny that this was the very mine which he stumbled upon so many years before.

Captain Dick Mine

THE OLD INDIAN who lived on Owl Creek—that waterway draining into Middle Lake from the Warner Mountains southeast of Alturas, California —was known as "Captain Dick".

Somehow, somewhere, he got hold of picture-rock gold, and there was born a legend that lives today in the high north country, more than a century and a quarter later.

Captain Dick might not have had enough savvy to spend his easy-come money wisely, but he did know enough not to tell where the gold came from. All that is known is that the "mine" was "on a mountain."

A pair of miners, operating on the theory that it would be easier to knock over Captain Dick than to make an original strike, apparently went after the old boy—and, so the story goes, came out losers.

In any event, white man's justice decreed that Captain Dick, an Indian who refused to share his wealth with the white man, must surely have shot the two miners with malice aforethought. Gold, not justice, was the law's chief concern in this case, and Captain Dick was tortured, finally killed. The secret of the gold mine did not escape his lips.

But, it still lived in his widow. The white man's code made a gentle turn here. Marriage—not killing—was the attempted fate. But, Mrs. Captain Dick said no, and she died true to her husband's secret.

Years pass, and then kerosene spills on the dying embers of the Captain Dick story. A shepherd lets it be known, through his actions and drunken words, that:

While driving his flock "between Pine Valley and Owl Creek" (according to the John D. Mitchell version in the November, 1941, *DESERT*) he spied an Indian emerging from a shaft. The redman, heavy bag in hand, paused long enough to close the mine entrance with a flat rock, and then ran on down the hill.

The shepherd found the tunnel "threaded with gold seam." What is more, for the next several months, that picture rock became his chief coin. For some time before he disappeared from the face of the earth, the herder visited the shaft whenever he needed more money for drink.

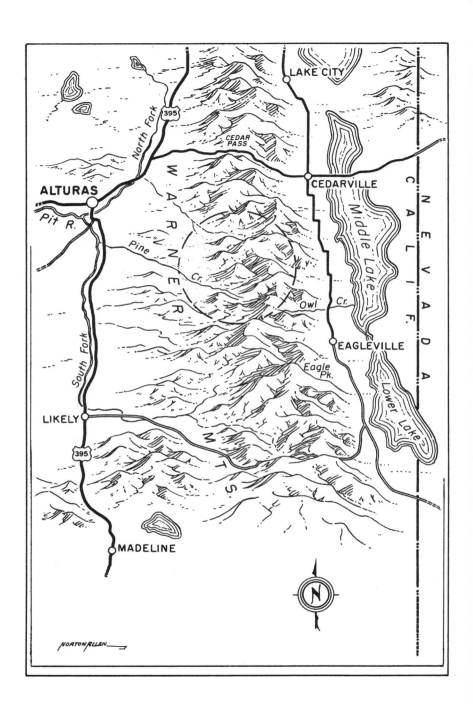

Tonto Quartz Vein

Two SHEPHERDS STUMBLED across the five skeletons on the northern slope of Mount Ord in the Tonto Basin country of Arizona.

Two of the skeletons were identified as the remains of a pair of discharged soldiers who had foolishly turned their backs on civilization (as represented by the Army post at Camp Reno) to find the source of the rich gold the Tonto Apache Indians had been trading to the white man for goods. The soldiers had last been seen alive in 1865—five years before the shepherds found their remains.

Among the bones and scraps of Army uniform was a large piece of white quartz "literally covered with bright yellow gold" (according to John D. Mitchell in the February, 1942, *DESERT*).

Henry Hardt of Chandler, Arizona, saw the specimen, and described it to Mitchell: "three inches long, two inches broad and at least one-third gold."

A somewhat similar story is told by Barry Storm in the January, 1955, *DESERT*. The soldiers are out of Ft. McDowell, and they make their strike in the Superstition Mountains—and it is here they die. They were somewhere in the region of the black-topped mountain which separates East Boulder and Needle canyons.

––––––––––

In DECEMBER, 1952, *DESERT* carried Kenneth E. Hickok's account of how a squad of U.S. Cavalrymen found a rich gold deposit in southern Arizona —and then lost it. The soldiers were chasing Apaches south from Maricopa Well on the Gila River, when they came across a pothole filled with water —and gold nuggets.

This lost gold is *really* lost. The author points to the "possible routes" in the Quijotoa or Baboquivari Mountains as the leading site candidates.

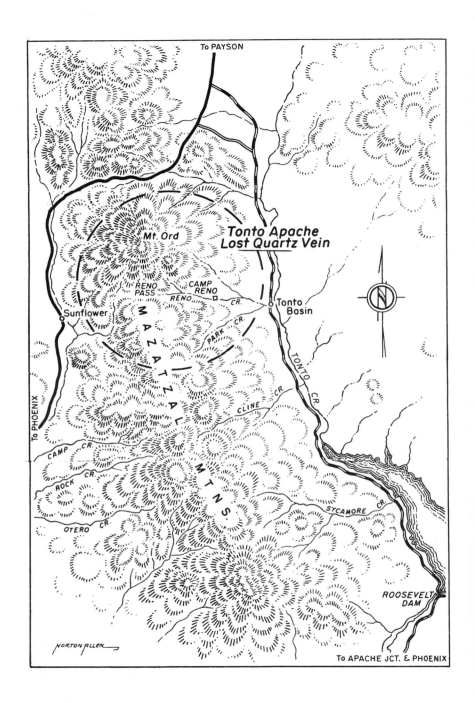

To PAYSON

Mt. Ord

Tonto Apache
Lost Quartz Vein

RENO
PASS
CAMP
RENO
RENO
CR.

Tonto
Basin

Sunflower

M
A
Z
A
T
Z
A
L

PARK
CR.

TONTO
CR.

CLINE
CR.

M
T
N
S.

CAMP
CR.

ROCK
CR.

OTERO
CR.

SYCAMORE
CR.

To PHOENIX

NORTON ALLEN

ROOSEVELT
DAM

To APACHE JCT. & PHOENIX

Organ Grinders' Ledge

An old Arizona prospector named Bill Bear told this yarn to John D. Mitchell, and Mitchell retold it in the November, 1942, *DESERT.*

The target area is Peeples Canyon west of Prescott, but the story opens further west near the Colorado River. Three Italian organ grinders, complete with crank-organs and trained monkeys, were hiking from LaPaz to Granite Creek, north of Prescott, in the early 1860s.

Somewhere along the long, long trail they came across an old Mojave Indian in great need of water. (The wonder is he did not die of shock, being met in mid-desert by three men, three organs, and three monkeys.)

The Italians shared their water, and when the Indian revived, he shared his great secret: gold . . . more gold than there were pebbles at their feet.

Where? "Two days' travel (quoting Bill Bear) across the burning sands brought them to the Santa Maria River, and on the third day they reached a deep canyon up in the hills north of Peeples Canyon."

It was there, all right—"the three Italians hurried westward and at a point a few hundred yards distance in a tributary arroyo a small ledge of dark colored rock arrested their attention . . . they broke off a piece, which glistened in the afternoon sunlight. It was thickly studded with gold."

The Italians worked all that night; next day they marked the place in their minds and on a crude map, and then hightailed it for civilization for food, water and tools.

But a band of Hualapais, bent on murder, became their fate. The Mojave and two of the Italians were slain. The third organ grinder, who had become temporarily separated from the group when the Hualapais struck, died of greed.

That is, he grabbed all the gold he could carry, but left room for only one full canteen of water. He struck out for Wickenburg and two days later, close to death, was found by a teamster named Francisco Gonzales.

To Gonzales the dying man told his story.

IN THE SAME general area is set the story of the Big Antelope Placer, told by Mitchell in the May, 1942, *DESERT*. "The Indians around Rich Hill laughed at the miners for wasting their time picking up what the Indians called small nuggets, when only a short distance away in the same country was another mountain known to them as 'Big Antelope' where the nuggets were larger and more plentiful."

Black Butte Gold

THIS IS A FIRST COUSIN to the Pegleg myth, concerning itself as it does with "black gold" on the Low Desert of California. There's also an Indian woman who "wanders into a railroad camp" (Glamis). Such a woman appears in some of the Pegleg yarns.

DESERT'S Black Butte story (August, 1943) was written by a 16-year-old boy, David Champion, who told about the experiences of his father, E. T. Champion, and two companions.

The Indian woman starts the legend in 1906 with her Glamis entrance. She gives one of the kind railroad workers her load of black rocks —just before she dies.

Two months pass and the rock is given a close look. It's gold, of course. The word gets out, and several people scout the nearby Chocolate Mountains southeast of Midway Well.

At the end of the first World War, Champion's father and two other men made a try to find the black butte, chief clue to the gold. The trio camped that first night "at a place that was then called Midway Wells."

Next morning they started off at daybreak. At six that morning they had a flat tire.

"While changing the tire, Dad went over to the other side of the car (the side away from the sun) to get a drink of water . . . As he raised the canteen to his lips he glanced idly over the desert and . . . right in front of him was the black butte."

They hiked to the butte, discovered a "large camp" at its base, poked around a mine tunnel that was badly caved, climbed the butte. The butte was "pure manganese" at its base, capped with a heavy growth of shrubs.

Unfortunately, the elder Champion and his companions were not able to capitalize on their discovery.

Prospector Ed Rochester of Winterhaven, wrote a letter to *DESERT* (October, 1943) in which he told about climbing a black butte on the mesa country north of the Cargo Muchacho Mountains in southeastern Imperial County.

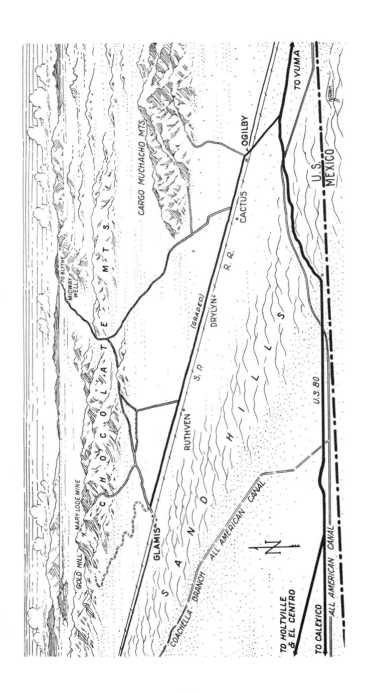

Josephine Gold Mine

WHEN THE GREAT DEPRESSION struck, Al Hainey was forced to sell newspapers to make a living. During these trying times the old man thought often of the gold horde he and a partner had come close to finding in the Henry Mountains of southcentral Utah. But, all he had to show for many months of hard prospecting in that rough country was a box of worthless mineral specimens. In fact, all he had found that could be converted into cash were some ancient Indian pots.

Hainey and his partner (a man of Spanish descent named Frank Olgean) had gone to Utah in 1900—with a waybill to the Lost Josephine —one of the oldest legendary mines in North America. The Josephine became lost when the small party of Spaniards had made the strike "somewhere to the north of Santa Fe"—and had later been frightened out of the country by Indians. This had taken place more than a century before Hainey's day.

Hainey and Olgean had picked-up the treasure map while prospecting in New Mexico. It led them not to the LaPlata or LaSal Mountains (chief candidates for the Lost Josephine locale) —but to the Henrys.

"After crossing the Colorado River at Escalante's old ford," wrote Charles Kelly in the October, 1943, *DESERT*, "they turned north to Fifty Mile Mountain, following a dim trail marked by small stone monuments. On the flat summit of the mountain, near a trail marker, they found a flat rock on which had been inscribed a large arrow. Following the direction of the arrow they discovered a hidden cave, on the back wall of which was a lengthy inscription in Spanish, giving further directions for reaching the mine. One of the landmarks indicated in the inscription was a series of three large round concretions, split open like halved apples. By sighting through the splits, approximate location of the mine could be seen."

The two prospectors found the landmarks and came to the place where the mine was supposed to be: "a small bench on the side of one of the smaller peaks of the Henrys, near a hidden spring."

Here were the ruins of an old smelter—there could be no mistaking it.

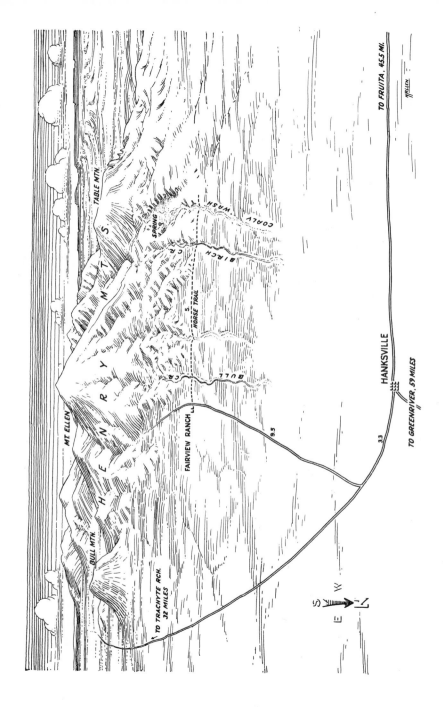

But, where was the gold-bearing vein? They searched for days. The fruitless days stretched into weeks and months.

Finally, Olgean quit for a sheepherding job. Hainey hung on for a bit longer, then he too left Utah. All he carried out of the Henrys were some Indian pots and the handful of rocks picked-up near the old smelter.

But, what of these rocks? Not until the newspaper-selling job drove him to near despair did Hainey have his specimens assayed. The report: estimated value of the ore: $50,000 a ton in gold!

Hainey, penniless and now 75 years old, started immediately for Utah. He hitchhiked and walked, and—suspicious of all men with whom he came in contact—finally disappeared from the face of the earth.

He was last seen by a herder named Harry Ogden near Hanksville.

A few days earlier, near Poison Spring Wash in Wayne County, author Kelly and his traveling companion, Frank Beckwith, had seen a small, elderly man walking down the dirt road toward the snow-capped Henry Mountains on the horizon. "Over his shoulder was slung a lightly filled gunny sack, and in one hand he carried a coffee pot half full of water." It was Hainey.

––––––––––

CHARLES KELLY (August, 1943, *DESERT*) described the work of Ed Wolverton, who had spent many years building a gold mill at the foot of the Henry's Middle Mountain. A small seam of gold-bearing rock had been unearthed on Middle Mountain around 1913, but it was low-pay, as Wolverton painfully discovered.

The Chinaman

WILLIAM CARUTHERS thought so much of this lost mine yarn that he went into the Panamints after it—and almost didn't come out.

The "Lost Chinaman" was the property of "Shorty" Harris of Death Valley, the best known prospector who ever set foot on the desert. Writing in the November, 1943, *DESERT*, Caruthers wisely let Shorty do the talking:

"I was working at Searles Lake for old man John Searles. One day I saw a fellow stagger down from the Slate Range and flop on the edge of the lake.

". . . it turned out he was a Chinaman who'd got sore at the boss over at Eagle Borax Works and started out afoot. The Paiutes told him about a short-cut over the Panamint, but he lost his way and ran out of water.

". . . he got the idea he was going to croak and wanted to get back to China . . . 'Salty Bill,' John Searles' teamster, was taking a load of borax to Mojave. So we threw the Chink on the wagon. I tossed his bag up and started away.

"The Chink called me back, dug into the sack, pulled out a piece of ore and gave it to me. I couldn't believe my eyes. It was damn nigh pure gold. Maybe 15 pounds.

"He tried to tell us where he'd found it. 'In the big timber,' he said, 'where a steep canyon pitches down into Death Valley.'

"John Searles and Salty Bill searched five years for that gold. No go."

Shorty tapped his breast. "I know," he said. "See that sawtooth? Over and down. There's your Lost Chinaman."

Shorty was just out of the hospital (and in his 70s) and half-way up the hill he gave out. Caruthers had to find help, but as it turned out it was a revived Shorty who led the younger man out of the mountain maze. The Lost Chinaman remains lost.

––––––––––

JACK STEWART, one of the last of the old burro prospectors, died in Darwin,

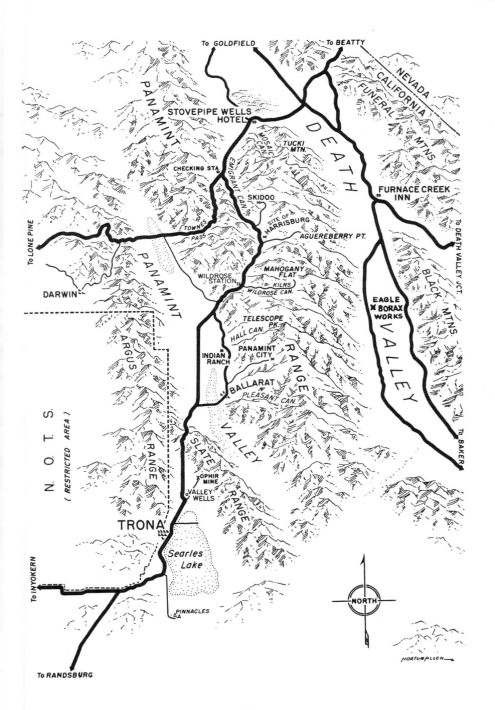

Calif., on May 16, 1947. A few days before he passed away, he told a secret to a friend—the story of Stewart's Ace-in-the-Hole ledge.

The article, not carrying a by-line because the author did not want to get "messed-up with goldhunters," was printed in *DESERT* for November, 1947.

Stewart's bonanza was born in 1897 during one of the prospector's foot trips in the Death Valley country. From Grapevine Canyon, near where Death Valley Scotty's Castle now stands, Stewart headed for Olancha via Stovepipe Wells, Townes Pass and Panamint Valley.

As Jack neared Stovepipe Wells on the east flank of the Panamints he was caught in a blinding rainstorm.

The downpour not only caused him to steer off course, it caused a slide in one of the canyons, unearthing a rich showing of gold-studded quartz float.

Two things are known: the canyon is on the Death Valley side of the Panamints; it is near Stovepipe Wells where Stewart had planned to camp that night.

Lost Arch Mine

THIS IS THE SECOND most popular California lost mine (Pegleg is first). The locale is the remarkably-formed Turtle Mountains lying north of Rice and west of Highway 95.

John D. Mitchell (*DESERT*, February, 1941) carries the tale back to the days of Mexican miners — a small party traveling east to LaPaz stumbling upon the placer ground in the Turtles. He wrote that they "sluiced out $30,000 worth of gold before the hot weather dried up the waterholes." (Mexican or U.S. dollars?) The Mexicans also built a two-room home whose main architectural feature was an arch. The arch, still standing, was the clue to the gold.

Writing in the November, 1944, *DESERT*, Walter Ford details his personal search for the treasure.

In 1883, a man named Amsden and an unnamed prospector from Needles left that town for a tour of the Turtles. A few weeks later, Amsden —more dead than alive—showed up at Goffs. He was alone, but his pockets bulged with gold.

When Amsden got his breath, he did the unexpected—he returned to his home in the East.

Ford knew "Mort" Immel of Barstow who knew "Dick" Colton of Goffs who helped Amsden when the gold-finder reached Goffs in his first encounter with civilization after his ordeal in the Turtles.

A few years after Amsden left the desert, Colton received a letter from him containing directions and a map to the placer horde.

"The mine is in the Turtle Mountains. The location is not far from a *natural* arch."

With this relatively good lead, Colton, Mort Immel and Herb Wit-mire went into the Turtles, but failed to spot the arch.

Ford picked-up another clue from an unnamed prospector in this country: "Once I find the arch with a large group of cacti closeby," the oldtimer told Ford, "my searching days are over."

During the war, Ford was visiting artist John Hilton, and the con-

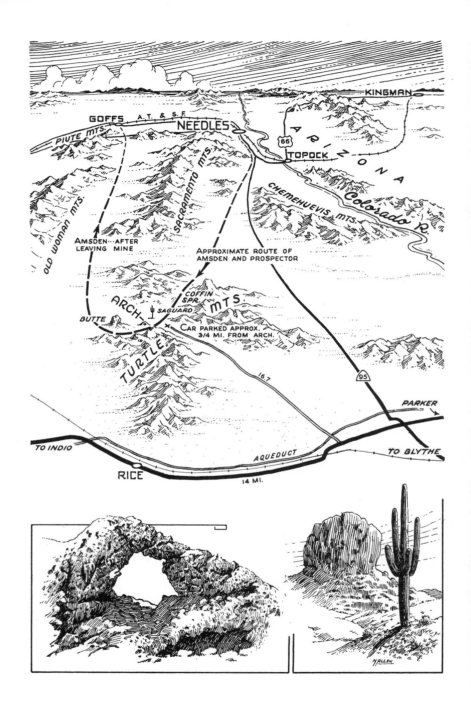

KINGMAN

GOFFS A.T. & S.F.

PIUTE MTS.

NEEDLES

66

TOPOCK

ARIZONA

SACRAMENTO MTS.

CHEMEHUEVIS MTS.

Colorado R.

OLD WOMAN MTS.

AMSDEN···AFTER
LEAVING MINE

APPROXIMATE ROUTE OF
AMSDEN AND PROSPECTOR

COFFIN
SPR.

ARCH

SAGUARO

MTS

BUTTE

CAR PARKED APPROX.
3/4 MI. FROM ARCH.

TURTLE

16.7

95

PARKER

TO INDIO

AQUEDUCT

TO BLYTHE

RICE

14 MI.

NALLEN

versation turned to lost mines and an unknown arch in the Turtle Mountains.

Hilton had never heard the lost mine part of the story—but he knew of a natural arch in the Turtles! He had spotted it while rockhunting in that range. Sure, he would be happy to take Ford to the arch—and he did.

While Hilton gathered prize rock specimens (carnelian, plume agate, geodes), Ford tramped around the arch looking for placer ground, or a likely place where Amsden and his partner could have cached a "tub half full of gold nuggets."

Ford found a saguaro in this unlikely habitat (could this have been the prospector's "group of cactus?"), but of gold there was no sign.

Mitchell adds this twist to the tale: the gold will be found in association with hematite.

Vallecito Gold

To HUGH RANKIN, a self-admitted "Tenderfoot with a capital T"— finding the lost gold of Vallecito would be easy.

Writing in the December, 1944, *DESERT*, Rankin described his advantages:

He had two knowledgeable partners, Alexander MacLeod and Theodore A. Higgins. The latter had invented a "radio finder" which would spot the buried gold; the former had learned the story of the lost treasure years before from a Diegueno Indian, and had already made one search on the spot (giving up after "running out of grub").

The story MacLeod told to Rankin was a simple one: After the Civil War killed the Butterfield Overland Stage, the adobe station at Vallecito was abandoned—temporarily. The new occupant, a former outlaw, set up house keeping with two ollas filled with gold, and a wife whom he later sent to Mexico City in search of better quarters.

During her absence, the householder was seen by a Diegueno Indian servant woman taking the gold off toward the southwest.

He was gone but a short time. "From the doorway of the old station the woman later saw the horse standing on a knoll in what was then known as Potrero Canyon. More recently the place has been known as Treasure Canyon."

The outlaw was killed in a runaway accident, and the Indian woman and her brother (the man who told the story to MacLeod) searched for the ollas—in vain. The outlaw's wife returned and also made a futile search.

Rankin, MacLeod and Higgins—"radio finder" notwithstanding— joined the roster of those who failed to find the gold.

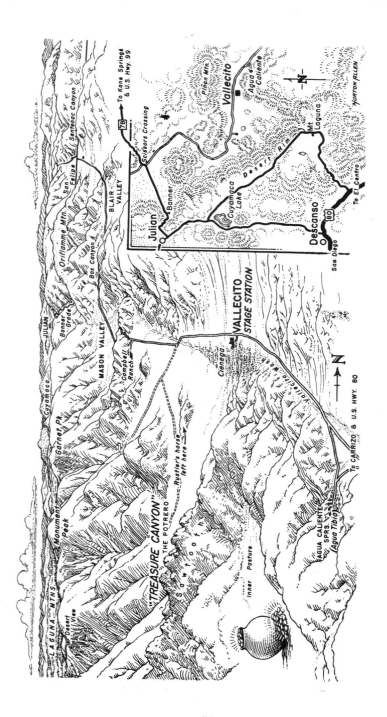

Wagoner's Rose Quartz

THE MAN'S NAME was Wagoner. The year: 1894.

Wagoner was a consumptive, and to continue living he had to spend as much time as possible in the Arizona outdoors. He walked and prospected and walked some more. An Easterner, little else is known about him. The story of his lost bonanza comes to us through a stage driver named Fred Mullins, who traveled the Pinal-Mescal run.

Wagoner was a regular passenger on Mullins' run. He would leave the stage out of Pinal and hike a big circle, prospecting along the way, strike the road and wait for Mullins to carry him back to Pinal.

One day Wagoner made a fabulous strike. He had been ". . . out of grub. Instead of making a long roundabout trip back past the western end of the Superstitions (wrote Barry Storm in the February, 1945, *DESERT*) . . . he headed straight across the country toward Pinal. He crossed the Salt River at Mormon Flat, hiked up the Apache Trail road to Tortilla Flat and then southeast up Tortilla Creek.

"For some hours he followed the creek bed between high cliffs and steep slopes until he reached fairly level country on the east side of Tortilla Mountain.

"Then he turned due south through the lower hills which, he knew, separated him from the head of La Barge Canyon and a trail that went on down the southern slopes of the Superstitions through Red Tank Canyon to Whitlow's Ranch near the road to Pinal beyond.

"Hiking for the better part of a day, Wagoner finally reached LaBarge Canyon where he found that he had misjudged his direction slightly and was a mile or so lower and farther west than he had expected to be . . ."

Night fell, but Wagoner walked another mile down the center of LaBarge Canyon. Next morning he took his bearings. He was "about three miles due east of Weaver's Needle . . ." and ". . . almost due north of Miner's Needle."

He began walking "over the broken hills to the east of Miner's Needle." In an hour's time he found the rose quartz vein outcropping—studded with gold.

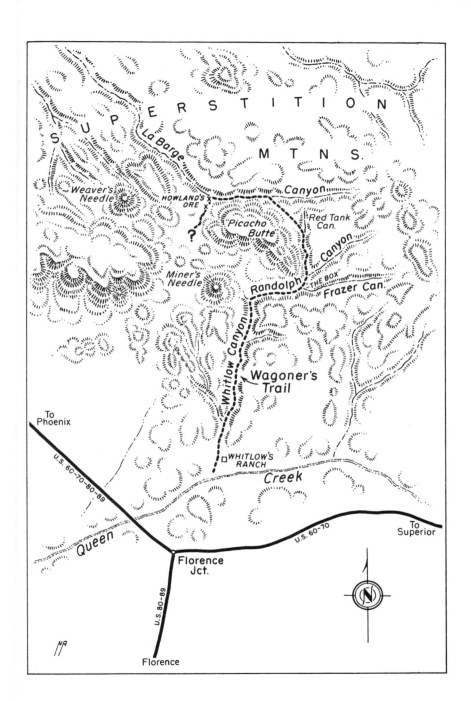

And now to the job of harvesting his bonanza. Wagoner did it the hard way. Bit by bit he carried out what he could on repeated and numerous trips stretching over the months. He rode Mullins' stage when he could, and the stage driver, of course, knew something was up—especially when it came time to hoist Wagoner's heavy pack aboard.

Wagoner, his fortune made, told Mullins his secret on what he announced was his last trip into the desert. He even drew a map, "showing the way back up Red Tank Canyon into upper La Barge Canyon and around a picacho butte."

And Wagoner provided another clue: he had planted a circle of trees around the outcrop.

But as far as Mullins was concerned, Wagoner might as well have left the trees unplanted, for Mullins never found his "legacy."

Peralta Dutchman

I HESITATE TO INCLUDE this yarn, for lost mine hunters have shown a tendency to become overly serious when considering the possibility of gold waiting for them in the fortress-sided Superstition Mountains of central Arizona. More than one man has died—several have been murdered—trying to rob the mountain of its treasure or supposed treasure. My guess is that the royalties I receive from this book will be the only hard cash that will be made from the Superstitions.

In Sonora a Mexican named Manuel Peralta lay on his death bed. Before he could go in peace to his heavenly reward, he had a secret concerning earthly reward that he felt compelled to tell his son. The young man, one Ramon Peralta y Gonzales, was recalled from Maricopa, Arizona, where he had been in residence a few short weeks.

When the boy returned to Maricopa, he had his dead father's treasure map in his pocket, and he needed a grubstake. He turned to an *Americano,* Charles M. Clark, Maricopa telegrapher.

Clark drove a hard bargain. A copy of the map in exchange for provisions, a horse and a rifle. Agreed; and Peralta Jr. was off to find the "X" on his father's map: "Clark saw that (the map) was an outline sketch of the Four Peaks on the north and of Weaver's Needle on the south and between the two a line had been drawn to intersect the . . . Salt River at a point about midway where the tributary canyon marked Fresco came into the river," wrote Barry Storm in the July, 1945, *DESERT.* "Four crosses were marked around the tributary junction with Fresco Canyon—and that magic word *mina!*"

The boy rode past the western edge of the Superstitions, through the pass at Apache Gap and on to the Salt River beyond at Mormon Flat. By following up the riverbank he came to the place of the two arrastres where his father had told him the placer gold lay.

Instead of arrastres, he stumbled across the bones of the Apache massacre which—26 years before—had driven his father from this country. Nearby were rotting sacks of gold concentrate taken from the unseen mine further up Fresco Canyon and apparently brought down to this camp for refining.

There was nothing greedy about young Peralta. He loaded the concentrate on his pack animal, and to hell with what treasures lay upcanyon. And

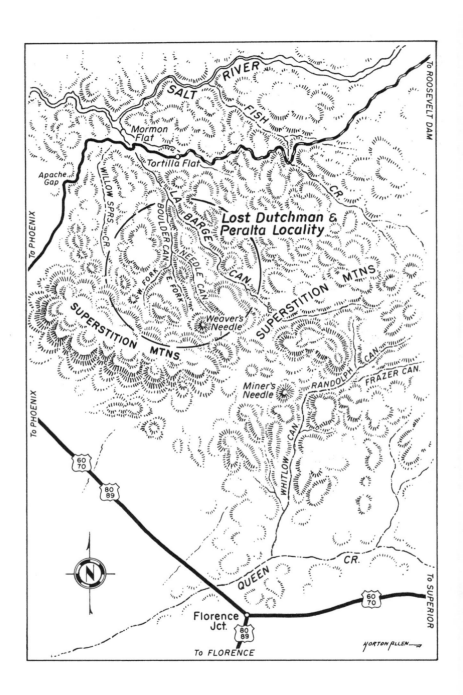

Peralta Jr. was honest. He gave Clark his share, and then hightailed it to California to live the full life.

Clark, of course, tried to find the right canyon—and failed. (Storm says Clark and his son concentrated their search "in LaBarge Canyon . . . entirely overlooking the fact that it is really a tributary of Tortilla Creek, coming into the latter near its mouth. To this day Tortilla Creek is still unrecognized as the true Fresco Canyon.")

Apparently Peralta Jr. lived too long—or at least outlived his gold. In 1930—56 years after finding his father's old camp—he returned to the Superstitions. This time he had no luck.

According to John Mitchell (*DESERT*, March, 1941) five Mexican miners (one of them being Peralta Sr.) escaped the Apache slaughter. These five men then spread the gospel of gold in the Superstitions throughout Sonora.

The original discovery of the mine (1846) by the Peralta brothers (Pedro, Ramon and Manuel) and their little band of family retainers, is detailed by Storm in the March, 1945, *DESERT*. The strike was made, says Storm, ". . . at the junction of the stream (LaBarge Creek) and the river (Rio Salado) ." This is the present site of Mormon Flat.

Pedro, the eldest brother, tracked the float to its source: ". . . higher and higher he climbed from La Barge onto Boulder Creek, on up Needle Canyon . . . There within a region from one to two miles northerly of a towering hat-shaped peak ("La Sombrera") . . . ."

From this point he made several forays into the mountain. ". . . finally high on the eastern slopes of a black-topped mountain a mile and a half due north of La Sombrera, he came upon rich twin outcrops of reddish, gold-bearing quartz. Circling around the same mountain he found (another bonanza) on the north side and still another below the southwestern slopes."

In Storm's Chapter II of the Peralta story, which was published by *DESERT* the following month (April, 1945) , we get these corroborating directions (supposedly given by Ramon Peralta to two prospector friends) : ". . . from the desert they would have to go up the first deep canyon from the western end of the range, climb northward over the backbone of the range itself until they came within sight of a huge sombrero-shaped peak dead ahead, travel downward past the base of the peak into a canyon (East Boulder) running northward until at last they found on the east side the entrance to a tributary canyon which was very deep, pot-holed and densely wooded with scrub oak. Then they were to turn about and go back southward up this tributary (Needle) canyon until they reached a point where the outlines of the hat-shaped peak to the south and the black-topped mountain to the west both matched from the same place the outlines upon the map. Near this spot they would find a marker upon the end of a rocky ledge. And the marker would be pointing to nearby mines!"

Who were Ramon's two friends? Jacobs, a German, and Ludi, a Hollander. Who shot them in the Superstition Mountains? Jacob Wiser and his partner, Jacob Walz. Who then shot Wiser? Walz—the Dutchman who has become the "darling" of the Phoenix Chamber of Commerce.

In Storm's Chapter III (May, 1945, *DESERT*) we see Walz grow wealthy—and old—too old to take anyone to his cache. Too old, even, to give directions to what was by then *The Lost Dutchman Mine*.

———————

In the following issue of *DESERT* (June, 1945), author Storm took readers into the same general area (LaBarge Canyon, Geronimo Head) for a look at "Rumors of Gold." This time we have Geronimo the master of the treasure, the key to which was "a certain spring at the foot of the mountain (in LaBarge Canyon) . . . By following the water" to its source the gold would be found.

And too (according to Storm) there's a mountain of solid silver hereabouts.

In the January, 1945, *DESERT,* Storm details the story of the "Soldiers Lost Vein of Gold" which bears a strong relationship to the "Tonto Quartz Vein" (page 39). Storm's soldiers do their prospecting—and dying—in the Superstitions.

John D. Lee's Mine

AFTER THE MOUNTAIN MEADOWS MASSACRE in 1857, John D. Lee was a hunted man. To escape the law and old friends, he headed into the recesses of Marble Canyon, making his headquarters at the ford of the Colorado River which became known as Lee's Ferry.

Every man who faced the virgin West became a miner of sorts, and indications are that Lee was a good prospector. With nothing but time on his hands, he devoted many years to exploring the rugged canyon of the Colorado.

A man with 19 wives must per force learn to keep his own counsel, and this Lee apparently did. The fact is, he made a rich strike somewhere in the Canyon, but told his wives nothing, and only let the secret out once.

Utah historian Charles Kelly pored over Lee's writings and found but a single reference to a mine. It came in a letter Lee wrote in prison after he had been brought to justice. The letter was written to one of his daughters about a year before his execution.

"I have just received a letter from Emma (one of the wives) and one from Judge Spicer," wrote Lee, "asking my permission to allow him horses to prospect with . . . and to tell him where those ledges was or is from which I brought some . . . I wrote back to them saying I did not want anything to do with Spicer's fortune hunting; that I wanted Ralph and John to cross the river and go to work at my place, the Mow Eabba (Lee's farm at Moenavi), lest someone would jump the claim and cause us trouble . . ."

Thus we know that even before his execution (in 1877), the legend of the Lee gold had been born.

The Kelly article on the Lost Lee appeared in the August, 1946, *DESERT*.

George Wharton James tells of a man named Brown (actually Isaac C. Haight, a leader, with Lee, of the Massacre) who made a search for the mine immediately following Lee's execution. (Even when faced with certain death, Lee would not divulge his secret—perhaps the unhappy man's only solace in the whole mismanaged affair.)

Robert B. Hildebrand, who as a 15-year-old had lived with Lee (in

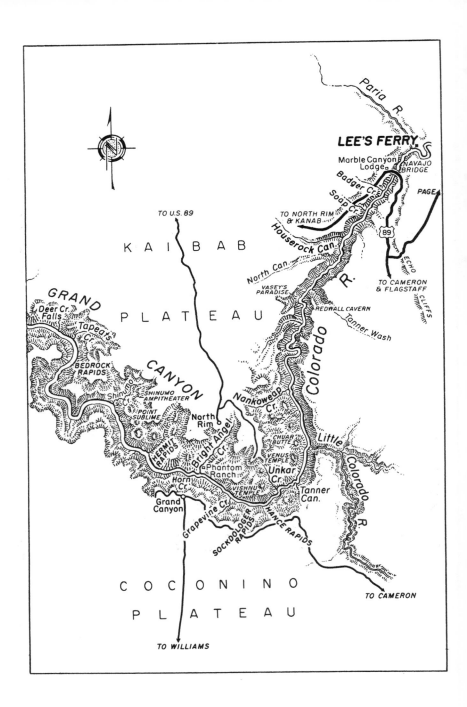

1875), told Kelly that he had "always believed Lee had found a rich mine somewhere in Grand Canyon."

Emma Lee moved to Holbrook, Arizona, after the funeral, and in due time married one Franklin French—a miner. French, of course, made a search for his almost-relative's gold mine, and in the process did do some good by helping build the French-Tanner Trail down to the Colorado near the mouth of the Little Colorado River. It was in this locale, too, that "Brown" had made his futile hunt (he looked for "seven cans of placer gold" supposedly buried by Lee).

Josiah F. Gibbs made up some fiction under the title of "Kawich's Gold Mine" in which is described a rich placer strike near the Grand Canyon's Vulcan's Throne. In later years, Gibbs confided in Kelly that the story was not entirely brought forth from his imagination—that he had indeed known the man who took out the Grand Canyon's gold.

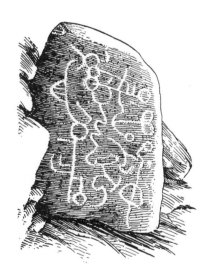

Silver in the Chocolates

"Dear Editor," began the letter received by *DESERT* in mid-1947. The writer, L. Harpending of Long Beach, Calif., went on to describe a quartz-silver outcropping he himself had found and then lost.

The low-eroded Chocolate Mountains on the east flank of Imperial Valley is the setting for Harpending's adventure. It began in 1920 when he accompanied a friend to the diggings of an old German prospector known as "Desert John." The camp was in the Chocolates about five miles northeast of Glamis.

Earlier, in Niland, the two newcomers had learned from a desert wanderer the approximate location of a spring of live water. After Harpending and his friend had looked over Desert John's ground, they decided to search for the spring.

"To describe the country we were in," wrote Harpending in the June, 1947, *DESERT*, "I am going to compare it to the wrist and fingers of a hand."

The two men had camped under a clump of paloverdes at the "wrist". Before them—like widespread fingers—stretched several dry washes running north into the Chocolate foothills.

Harpending went up one wash, his friend another. They met at the head of the washes, and then headed back to their camp via two different washes.

" . . . I was about two-thirds of the way back when I ran into a large ledge of quartz," wrote Harpending.

He chipped off samples and put them in his pack. "It looked mineral-bearing to me."

Harpending did not know just how "bearing" his samples were until Los Angeles assayer John Herman reported that the handful of quartz contained 32 ounces of silver and a trace of gold.

"I felt very much elated over my find and decided to go back in a few days and locate it, as it was on government land."

But, fortune in the form of a job offer intervened. Harpending went to Plumas County to manage a 10-stamp mill.

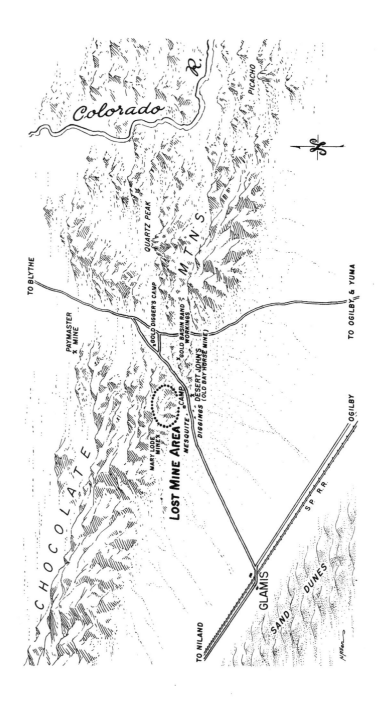

It was three years before Harpending had an opportunity to test his memory. After a week "of the hardest days I ever put in," he gave up.

Eighteen months later he tried again—with the same discouraging results. At this time he learned that Desert John had been murdered and his cabin burned to the ground. Rumor had it that the old German was killed for his cache of gold dust.

On this same trip, Harpending located an old silver mine in the area that had been worked in the 1890s. Its 150-foot shaft was caved, but samples picked up near the main pit assayed $80 to the ton. But, Harpending was not able to follow the vein to the silver outcrop he had stumbled upon in the wash. He surmised that a cloudburst had changed the wash's topography and probably covered the vein.

Three more attempts were made in the next 10 years: no luck.

"It is worth looking for, and if I were 10 years younger, I would try my luck again," concluded Harpending.

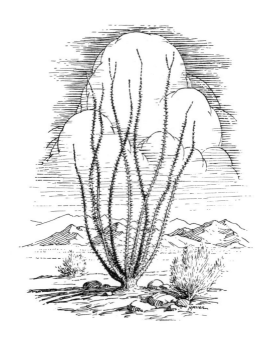

Wright's Treasures

I Include Richard Van Valkenburgh's personality sketch of prospector Fred Wright (*DESERT*, Sept., 1947) in this lost treasure compilation because of the value of the map that accompanied the article.

Wright, who "used the tail of his burro for a compass," roamed the length and breadth of the Arizona - Sonora border country where the water-holes are few and far between.

He stored in his soul the lore of the bonanzas supposedly lost along the historic camino, and admitted to doing a little digging himself. Apparently he concentrated on the "buried treasure" of San Marcelo, a mission founded in 1699 for the Papagos by Padre Kino (number 6 on the map).

John Mitchell Details one version of Sonoyta's lost treasure in the June, 1941, *DESERT*. He has a Father Miguel Diaz prospering in the "green vale of the Sonoyta," growing rich with much gold. "The large church and all the buildings were painted white and presented a beautiful sight . . ."

The Padre sends out prospecting parties for more mines, which they find. But all this doesn't make Fr. Diaz a better man—in fact he is very decidedly a bad man and finally he pushes the Papagos too far. In 1750 they revolt and massacre the Christians in Sonoyta, Carborca, Bac and Guevavi. The bodies of Fr. Diaz and two other priests were "thrown into the underground room with the gold and the walls and the roof of the church were thrown down." As of today, the gold still awaits a discoverer, and the priests' bones still await more formal burial.

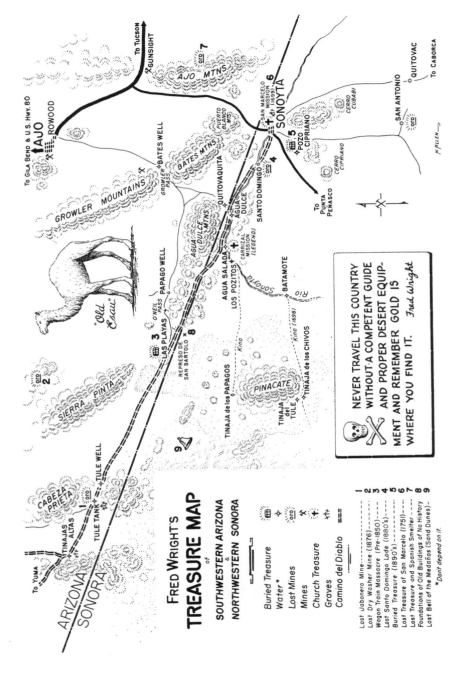

FRED WRIGHT'S
TREASURE MAP
of
SOUTHWESTERN ARIZONA
&
NORTHWESTERN SONORA

Buried Treasure
Water*
Lost Mines
Mines
Church Treasure
Graves
Camino del Diablo

1 — Lost Jabonero Mine ----------------
2 — Lost Dry Washer Mine (1876) ----------
3 — Wagon Train Massacre (Pre-1850) -----
4 — Lost Santo Domingo Lode (1880's) -----
5 — Buried Treasure (1890's) ------------
6 — Lost Treasure of San Marcelo (1751) ---
7 — Lost Treasure and Spanish Smelter ----
8 — Foundations of Old Buildings of No History --
9 — Lost Bell of the Medaños (Sand Dunes) --

*Don't depend on it.

NEVER TRAVEL THIS COUNTRY WITHOUT A COMPETENT GUIDE AND PROPER DESERT EQUIPMENT AND REMEMBER GOLD IS WHERE YOU FIND IT. *Fred Wright*

Turquoise Shrine

ONCE WHILE DISCUSSING Navajo folklore and its remarkable closeness to reality, John Wetherill remarked: "I don't know why or how these things be. I only know they are."

And so they are for an Indian trader named Toney Richardson who told *DESERT* readers (February, 1948) about an indelible incident that happened in his life.

Everyone in Navajoland had heard about a turquoise shrine — an altar upon which the ancients gave offerings of the Southwest's "blue diamonds." Some years ago an old Navajo friend, Todachene Nez, went to the shrine with Richardson.

They rode "three miles to the rim of Navajo Canyon. Another three miles down a scenic trail into Neetsin Canyon brought me to the foot of the cliff in which Inscription House cliff ruins is situated . . . Todachene Nez . . . led off. We covered only a short distance before halting at the base of a great rock towering better than 125 feet above the canyon floor" — the turquoise shrine! Richardson was as surprised and unbelieving as the most casual observer would be — the shrine is within the monolith, a subterranean cavern entered from the top of a great rock through a passage 8 to 10 feet wide.

Within it murderous depths

(several men had lost their lives trying to steal its treasure) was an underground geyser. This water periodically boiled up into the cavern. Into this terrible hole the ancient Indians had thrown turquoise offerings to appease whatever god caused the horrible roaring sounds that came from the depths of the rock.

Richardson and his friend picked-up several drilled pieces of turquoise on the rock that day, but they were not equipped (nor did they have the desire) to explore underground.

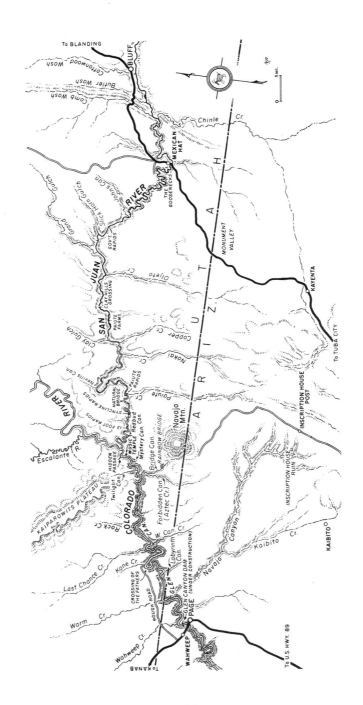

Tim Cody's Ledge

THIS JUNE, 1948, STORY marks the initial *DESERT* appearance of Harold O. Weight as a lost mine researcher. Weight is without peer in this category today.

"Tim" Cody's story takes place in 1908 in Nevada. "Tim should not have been a prospector, since he lacked the most important single qualification for the job—a good sense of direction," wrote Weight. "Tim could lose himself even when sober—and he was not always sober."

He carried a little water, but no food. Fifteen miles is not a great distance. But, between Tim's camp at Stewart Springs and Golddyke lies an eroded prehistoric lake bed. Tim wandered in and out of the ravines— and as the sun sank, he was lost. " . . . he found himself at the foot of a knoll covered with junipers," wrote Weight. "Hoping to orient himself, he climbed to the top of the knoll."

He recognized two landmarks: Paradise Peak, north and east of Golddyke; and, westward near Rawhide, the black pyramid called Pilot Cone.

The landmarks brought a welcome sense of relief, for now he was no longer lost. So he sat down, lit his pipe, and looked around. At his feet was an outcrop of white quartz stained with iron.

No prospector—professional or amateur—can resist a piece of quartz. Tim took hammer to it, and every piece he cracked revealed gold.

Gold fever hit Tim like a ton of—gold. It destroyed his capacity to reason. He had to get to town right now! To spend the night on the golden hill was unthinkable. He had to make his claim among his fellow men —*immediately.* He savagely struck his pick into a nearby tree to "mark the spot," and then set off for Golddyke.

"I seemed to kind of go blind," he is reported to have said. At the end of three days of wandering, he found himself at the abandoned Pactolus Mine, less than 10 miles from his camp at Stewart Springs.

At the mine he found water and food—and immediately resumed his quest for Golddyke. This time he made it. But he was never able to retrace his steps to the knoll of gold.

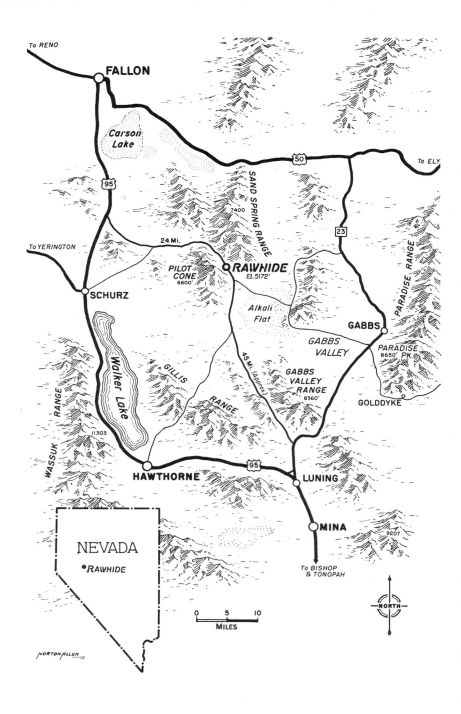

To RENO

FALLON

Carson
Lake

To ELY

SAND SPRING RANGE

7400

95

24 Mi.

To YERINGTON

PILOT
CONE
6600'

RAWHIDE
El. 5172'

23

PARADISE RANGE

SCHURZ

Alkali
Flat

GABBS

GABBS
VALLEY

PARADISE
8650' PK.

GILLIS

Walker Lake

45 Mi. (approx.)

RANGE

GABBS
VALLEY
RANGE
8360'

GOLDDYKE

WASSUK RANGE

11303

HAWTHORNE

95

LUNING

NEVADA

•RAWHIDE

MINA

9207

To BISHOP
& TONOPAH

0   5   10
MILES

NORTH

NORTON ALLEN

— 74 —

Cerro Colorado Silver

TREACHERY, INTRIGUE, MURDER, the gods' curse—and $70,000 in silver—are mixed into the legend surrounding a supposed treasure near Arivaca, south of Tucson.

The story begins a few years before the Civil War when an American Army Major, Sam Heintzelman, walked into Solomon Warner's general emporium in Tucson. On the counter was a piece of lustrous gray ore—stromeyerite ("silver-copper glance"). Heintzelman lives in Mexican folklore as a Yankee villain. While outwardly maintaining a casual air, he was burning inside to know where the ore had come from. The trail he followed with the instincts of a bloodhound led to a Mexican named Ouidican, a teamster.

The bargain—sworn to in public—struck between the two men was this: Ouidican would lead Heintzelman to the ore's source for $500 in gold and a half-interest in the mine.

Ouidican took the American to the base of a small reddish mountain known as El Cerro Chiquito, south of the Cerro Colorado Mountains and north of Arivaca.

There in a crude shaft, evidently worked by Sonorans in days past, was more of the ore—a seemingly endless supply.

The "partners" returned to Tucson and Heintzelman settled his debt —not with the $500 promised, but with a *boleta* of Tubac papermoney worth 50c!

"This," said Heintzelman, "is enough to pay a damned Mexican."

Writer Richard Van Valkenburgh (*DESERT*, Sept. '48) uncovered this half of the story in Saric, Sonora. He then visited the ruins of the Cerro Colorado Mine where the second half of the tale was revealed to him by Charles E. Udall, who had lived on the ground since 1905.

Heintzelman sank a 50-foot shaft at the site in 1856. A few months after he began his mining career, however, he was run off the property by the brothers Thomas and Ignacio Ortiz, owners of the Rancho La Aribac, which embraced the mine site. The Ortiz boys sold out to the Sonora Mining and Exploring Company. Charles D. Poston (a name famous in Arizona history) was boss of the operation.

In 1860 the pot boiled over. A cave-in killed 15 Mexican-Indian miners and ruined the underground workings; American troops were withdrawn from the area and the Apaches filled the vacuum; and Poston's brother, John, shot and killed his Mexican foreman, Juanito, as the latter tried

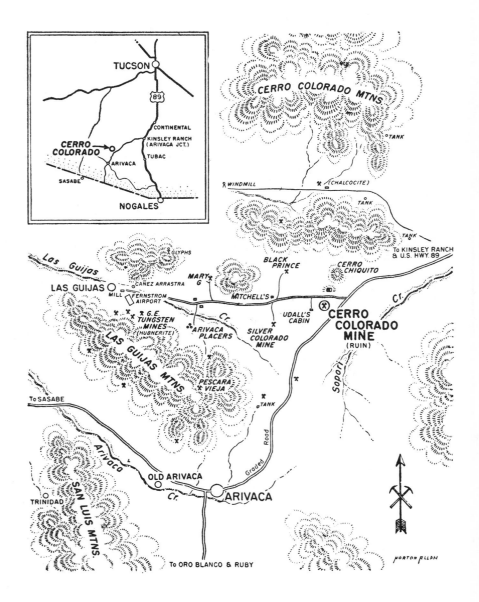

to make it across the border with a string of mules ladened with silver ore.

With Juanito's death, the remaining miners mutineed, stole every bit of property they could tear from the foundations, and bore it to Mexico.

They also brought home a story; somewhere on the slope between the shaft of the Cerro Colorado and the Cerro Chiquito, Juanito had buried $70,000 in silver bullion.

A band of Sonoran outlaws raided the mine soon after. They killed John Poston and two Germans, and leveled what was left of the Cerro Colorado Mine works in an effort to find Juanito's legacy.

————————

THE CERRO COLORADO country is also the setting for the Lost John Clark Silver Mine, a John D. Mitchell yarn (April, 1947, *DESERT*).

Clark, a Missourian, was in this country at the time of the troubles detailed above (Mitchell has Apaches, not Sonora outlaws, swooping down on the small ranchers and miners).

Clark had 40 tons of rich ore awaiting shipment to the mill (in St. Louis, Missouri!) when the Apache troubles became intensified. The St. Louis caravan surely would not get through, so Clark threw the ore back into the mine shaft and pulled the timbers out from the entrance. Estimated 1861 value of the silver: $80,000.

The late Mrs. Mary Black, wife of a pioneer Santa Cruz County jurist, told Mitchell of having seen Clark's stockpile. The shaft, she remembered, was "some distance from the Heintzelman Mine . . . on one of the great fault fissures along which the rich ore bodies of the district are found."

Clark fled to Tucson with the surviving white men of the district. He then went East where he died. Silver was demonetized and most of the old workings were forgotten.

Pegleg

MENTION "PEGLEG" TO A California desert dweller, and the first thought apt to spring to his mind is "gold"—not *gold* gold, but *black* gold.

In 1852 one-legged John O. Smith, traveling from Yuma to Los Angeles via Warner's Ranch, left the beaten track somewhere east of Warners and struck for a more direct route to the ranch. Smith, a good horsetrader and guide but a poor mineralogist, picked up some dark heavy pieces of what he thought were "native copper" specimens somewhere on his "shortcut to Warners." The black lumps of rock were found atop "one of three hills."

In Los Angeles he showed his desert curiosities to a friend who did know his metals and minerals. The assay: pure gold coated with "black desert varnish."

Needless to say, our hero tried in vain to return to his hill of gold. How hard did he try?

One version of the old tale (told in the November, 1946, *DESERT* by the most famous of all latter-day Pegleg searchers, Henry E. W. Wilson) has Smith "disappearing forever." In the meantime, news of his find filters through frontier Southern California.

In 1876 fuel is heaped on the smoldering tale of the "burned black gold of the Pegleg" when an Indian woman staggers into the Southern Pacific Railroad's end-of-line construction camp at Salton in the basin of the same name.

Wilson puts it this way: ". . . she and her buck started from the reservation at the head of the Rio San Luis Rey to go to the Cocopah Reservation near Yuma. Their canteen leaked, and the man had died of thirst. She wandered two days in search of water. Once she climbed one of the *tres picachos* and from there saw the smoke of the construction train."

Atop the *pichacho* she picked up some heavy black rocks which she later gave to one of the railroad men. The woman then disappeared.

A few years later, a half-breed laborer at Warner's Ranch found the golden hill. He died before he could make too many trips into the back-

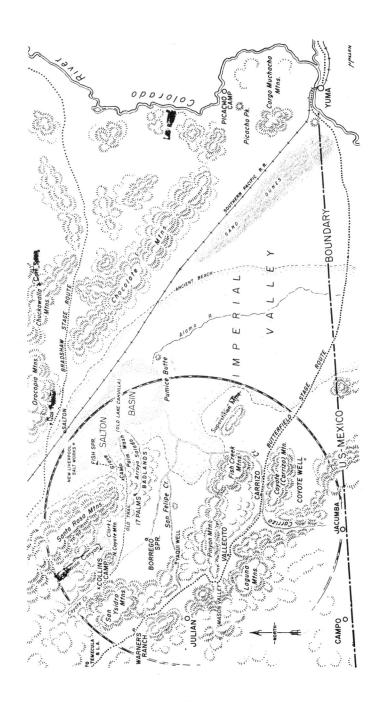

country, but his wife, who had been with him on one of his gold-gathering jaunts, related one clue: their base camp was the "Spring of the White Ledge."

More "secrets" from Wilson, this time in the October, 1948, *DESERT*:

Around the turn of the century, Wilson and John Collins made a concerted search for the Pegleg Mine. Wilson, describing himself as "green as grass" remembered seeing the top of three hills "somewhere between 17 Palms and Fish Springs," with the middle one appearing as if it were covered with black rock. But Wilson did not climb it, for Collins had momentarily disappeared with his burros, and, afraid of becoming lost, Wilson tracked him down.

"I believe one reason why the Pegleg gold was never found is that the searchers have been looking for large hills instead of low ones," Wilson remarked, adding: on a ridge on the south side of Grave Wash is the only site on the Colorado Desert where he has ever found *black* petrified wood. Scattered practically everywhere else on this desert are specimens of dull brown and tan petrified wood (rarely of gem grade). Does the chemistry of Grave Wash suggest something of significance?

There is another side to the Pegleg coin. Some say he was a fall-down drunk who had quickly learned that the best way to get free drinks was to tell his transient patrons what they wanted to hear: a crazy tale about the desert and three hills and black gold. As the legend of his supposed discovery spread, it was easier and easier to find men willing to buy a free drink to hear from the very lips of the famous Pegleg Smith the story of the golden horde by then familiar to men from San Francisco to San Diego. Why, there

17 Palms

was a man in Bakersfield who had a cousin in Yuma who knew a man who actually shook hands with old Pegleg!

Pegleg enjoyed his local fame and the liquor it brought him. Why curb the rumor?

All this is the theory advanced by James A. Jasper in the March, 1957, *DESERT*. Jasper, who represented the Borrego area as a San Diego County Supervisor prior to establishment of Imperial County, was a student of the Pegleg facts, and his evidence is convincing.

For what it is worth, my inclination is to go along with this version of the Pegleg story. He found riches in the Borrego Badlands, but it was not gold—it was a marketable story that grew into a legend.

However, I am with the minority in my evaluation of Pegleg. I doubt if any other single subject has drawn as much attention from *DESERT* readers as has the Pegleg story. Everyone, it seems, has an opinion or a clue to offer. Here, briefly as possible, are some of the appendages to the Pegleg story which have appeared in *DESERT*:

July, 1940—A brief item reports that a prospector named Jackson Hill claims he found Pegleg's mine in the Chuckawalla Mountains, 14 miles south of Desert Center, Calif. Hill followed a map he had gotten 36 years earlier in Alaska.

August, 1940—John D. Mitchell has Pegleg in the Bullion Mountain country between Bagdad and Twentynine Palms, on the Mojave Desert (see story on page 24).

September, 1940—Letter from Bradley R. Stuart (who passes along a sage aside: ". . . the only difference between a prospector and a jackass is two legs and a few inches on the ears"). Stuart calls Jackson Hill's find in the Chuckawallas so much "baloney." Stuart's partner's father and Smith were friends. Smith told him: "She's in no ledge. I pick her up out of the dirt in a little valley high in the mountains . . ."

October, 1940—Jackson Hill takes a swing at Stuart, and reveals details of his Alaska map. It was given him in 1912 by one Dutch Sholtz who said he had been Smith's partner. They made their strike while driving burros and horses along "the Bradshaw stage line to Corn Springs."

November, 1940—H. E. W. Wilson jumps into the Pegleg picture, reminding all concerned that there were two Pegleg Smiths! The given name of one was John O.; the other was Thomas. The former found the black nuggets; the latter had a mine "contiguous to the Chocolate Mountains."

November, 1946—Letter from O. H. Eddy of Calipatria, Calif., who claims to be the great-nephew of Lazarus Smith—the "true" Pegleg. Eddy says Lazarus was an honest, respectable man who took his gold nuggets back to

Penn, Michigan, with him. The slander connected to Smith's name is laid to a one-legged outlaw who posed as the gold discoverer. According to Eddy, "the proper location (of the Smith placer) is not far from the old Spanish Trail on the Mojave Desert."

March, 1947—Letter from W. C. Henneberger, Grand Junction, Colorado. ". . . I would place it northwest of Glamis, 10 or 15 miles, and toward the Chocolate Mountains."

October, 1947—Letter from Harold Withrow, El Paso. Withrow wrote that Harry A. Pitts was in Nevada ("16 or 17 miles northwest of Indian Springs") in 1907 when he came across a miner who had lost his burros. The man had "found the Lost Pegleg," and had 20 sacks of ore—but no burros. Pitts did the hauling in his wagon in exchange for one of the sacks of ore. Much later he sold the sack's contents for $2300.

December, 1947—Louis Kellerhals, giving his source as Fig Tree John, says Pegleg got all his gold from his Mohave Indian wife. The bride took it from tribal stores—but was not permitted to tell her husband the whereabouts of the Mohave's placer ground. Pegleg ran off to Los Angeles to sell the gold he had been given; later his wife followed him—it was she who stumbled into Glamis, nearly dead and with a shawl full of black nuggets.

July, 1949—Philip Bailey's *Golden Mirages* is quoted. In 1855 Pegleg was rescued at the San Felipe station on the Butterfield Stage Line. He was taken to Warner's Ranch where he told about the gold find.

May, 1950—Were the "heavy black stones" that freighter Charlie Brooks threw at his team the same stones that gave Pegleg his fame? Brooks operated on the Chihuahua to Los Angeles route. The rocks came from the Vallecito Desert area. Nothing beat them for throwing. Only they were pure gold, as was determined years later when an assay was made on a couple of the stones which had gotten home in Brook's pocket. Brook's told his story to his granddaughter, Maggie, who sifted the evidence and came to the conclusion that Charlie's throwing rocks most likely will be found "near Yuma, perhaps in the Chocolate Mountains, but perhaps, too, south of the International Boundary." None of the old jerkline trails passed through the Vallecito area. Charlie Brooks did a lot of freighting on the route "east of Yuma along the Gila River to Agua Caliente." By either of two routes, he traveled to and from his shipping point in Chihuahua through . . . Organ Pipe Cactus National Monument."

February, 1951—The John D. Mitchell version. Mitchell believes the lost buttes are located near the point where the eastern ends of the Chuckawalla and Chocolate mountains converge, on the north side of Salton Sea. Mitchell prospected the area, found the butte, and gathered up some of the gold specimens lying about on the ground! Only Mitchell was out looking for meteorites on this trip, and he picked up the "brown hematite" specimens out of habit. Later (20 years), he found out that they contained gold. Mitchell believes his find is "another of those rare chimneys that have always produced so much gold."

April, 1951—Letter from Bob Sanfley. The writer recalled an old Chemehuevi Indian who knew where the three buttes lay; a short distance off the trail "formerly used by the Indians, which ran from old Fort Mojave to San Diego."

May, 1954—Henry Splitter details the systematic search prospector Tom Grover made for the Pegleg, as described in the Riverside newspaper in 1884. Grover made a great study of the Pegleg evidence, and pinpointed his search in the Borrego country. In all he made five trips into the desert, generally working the areas adjacent to the Borrego Badlands. On his fifth trip he disappeared from the face of the earth.

January, 1956—During World War II, John Marston meets a soldier who had found 20 pounds of nuggets in a cave in the Borrego Springs - Seventeen Palms area—the Borrego Badlands.

August, 1957—Walter Ford quotes Major Horace Bell (1870) : "The author has little faith in the actual existence of the Pegleg mine, because it was reported by that artistic old liar, Pegleg Smith, whom he had the honor of knowing . . . he (Smith) sat around the old Bella Union Bar, telling big lies and drinking free whiskey . . ."

The Old Overland Stage Station at Vallecitos
Before Its Restoration.

Hassayampa Flood

As A Sidebar to a story on the 1949 Caballeros Trail Ride (an annual event in Wickenburg, Arizona), Randall Henderson told about a lost treasure in the upper Hassayampa River bed. The article appeared in the July, 1949, *DESERT*.

South of the old mining town of Wagoner, the hills close in and the river flows through a narrow portal of rock—a perfect damsite.

No Westerner, it seems, can pass up a perfect damsite, and so in 1889 a large dam was built here—the only attempt ever made to plug the Hassayampa.

Wrote Will C. Barnes: "February 22, 1890 . . . the dam burst, carrying death and destruction to those living below. Over 70 lives were lost and heavy damage suits ensued. Dam was built primarily for hydraulic mining."

Added Henderson: "The loss of the dam gave rise to one of Arizona's lost treasure stories. The tale is that a safe was washed downstream and never recovered, although it was said to contain a small fortune in gold dust, and fortune hunters searched for years along the bed of the stream in an effort to locate it."

Perhaps today's modern metal detectors would do well here.

————

On September, 13, 1913, the booming Nevada mining town of Goldfield suffered a devastating flashflood. The water rolled off the rimrocks west of town and came roaring through the main part of Goldfield. Two persons were killed, scores of houses and business buildings were crumbled, and the water carried before it all manner of personal property.

Included in the still-buried property are a couple of safes, jewelry, cookie jars full of gold coin, fat purses, plus a sampling of everything else the well-appointed 1913 Western boom town home and store might have contained. My story was carried in the May, 1962, *DESERT*.

A few years ago while digging post holes, a Goldfield man unearthed a case of beer. I have found many old bottles in this town—but all were empty.

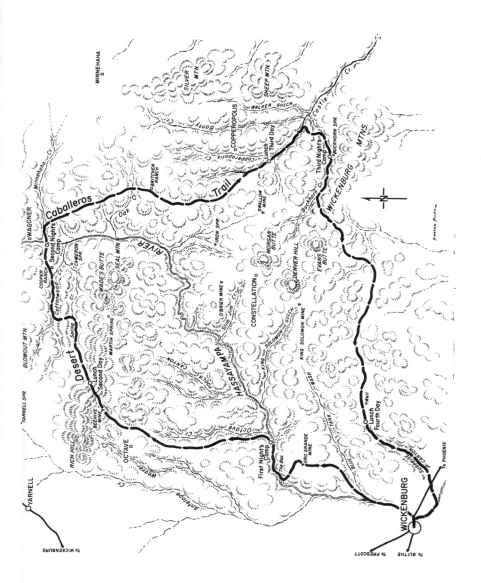

The Breyfogle - Amargosa

THE MYSTERIOUS AMARGOSA country fringing Death Valley is bisected by California Highway 127 running from Baker to Shoshone, Death Valley Junction and Nevada. This was the very route taken by California-bound horsetraders (and horse thieves), trappers, soldiers, colonizers and gold-seekers. It is said the first miners to do a little dry panning in the sands of Salt Creek were Spaniards (1826-30). They were successful, and, as these things usually happened, the years passed, a mine was developed and abandoned and redeveloped. The Indians did some killing and chasing-off to add blood to the gold from the Amargosa Mine. As late as February, 1950, *DESERT* told of the efforts of one Jack Moore, then engaged in trying to squeeze more gold out of the old mine. Many owners, many stories . . . an amazing amount of not-so-concrete facts concerning one of West's oldest mining operations.

Writing in the issue of *DESERT* mentioned above, John L. Von Blon gives an interesting sidelight on Anton Breyfogle, whose name is synonymous with "Death Valley Lost Mine" (see below). George Rose, superintendent of the Amargosa in the middle 1860s declared that the golden specimens Brey-fogle showed to the world were highgrade from the Amargosa. (Breyfogle spent a day at the mine.) Another mine expert, Frank Denning, examined the Breyfogle nugget and declared it to be Amargosa mine ore. Gold-in-matrix —like a fingerprint—is individualistic and unique.

But, there is much more gold on the Amargosa. In 1872, wrote Von Blon, a Bishop resident, "Johnny" McCloskey, went to Texas to get married. A few years later he and his bride piled all their worldly belongings onto a light wagon and hit the trail to California. At Marl Spring one of their two horses died. The McCloskeys had no choice. They abandoned the wagon, packed absolute necessities on the live horse, and set off for Ash Meadows— 140 miles distant.

One evening they camped "on the Amargosa River, 30 or 40 miles above the mine." There McCloskey saw a "natural embankment of black boulders on a broad, lengthy sand flat." In an hour of panning, he had an ounce and a half of gold.

Later, when he and his bride were safe at home, McCloskey returned

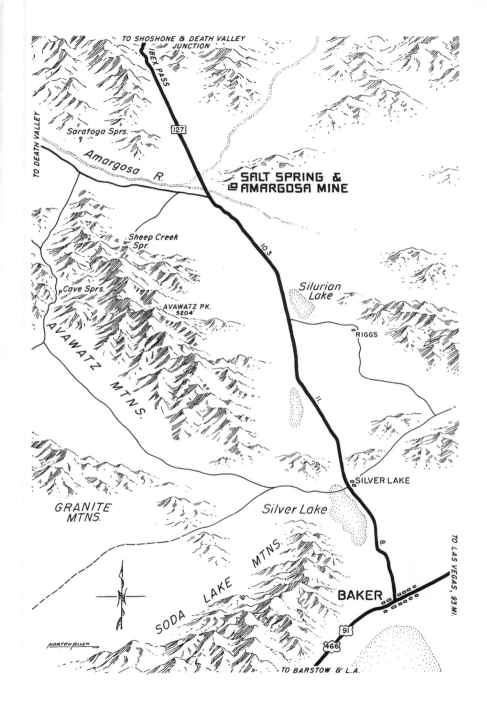

TO SHOSHONE & DEATH VALLEY
JUNCTION

IBEX PASS

127

TO DEATH VALLEY

Saratoga Sprs.

Amargosa R.

SALT SPRING &
AMARGOSA MINE

Sheep Creek
Spr.

10.3

Silurian
Lake

Cave Sprs.

AVAWATZ PK.
5204'

RIGGS

AVAWATZ MTNS.

GRANITE
MTNS.

SILVER LAKE

Silver Lake

SODA LAKE MTNS.

8.

BAKER

TO LAS VEGAS, 93 MI.

NORTON ALLEN

91

466

TO BARSTOW & L.A.

to the Amargosa accompanied by "Steve" Golden. The abandoned wagon had been looted—and while they found plenty of black boulders along the sandy streambed, the rich placer eluded them.

Golden, who died at age 90 in 1945, made several searches for the placer ground. His son, George, told Von Blon he was not planning to give up. That was in 1950.

Breyfogle came into this country in 1863, according to John D. Mitchell (September, 1940, *DESERT*). In company with prospectors O'Bannion and McLeod, he stopped off at a ranch in Las Vegas in southern Nevada. From there, the partners headed south.

When Breyfogle returned to Las Vegas, he was alone and his skull was fractured.

Three days out of Las Vegas, recounted Breyfogle, the trio had made camp "at a small spring high up on the side of a mountain range at the end of a narrow box canyon."

Into this camp came three Paiutes with good tidings: three miles from camp was a rich ledge of gold. The Indians took Breyfogle to the gold—and then tomahawked him. When Breyfogle regained consciousness, he made his way back to camp and discovered the murdered bodies of his partners.

In *DESERT's* September, 1953, issue, James P. Kelm says *Louis Jacob* Breyfogle and his two companions were attacked by Indians "while they were camped at a point believed to be near the base of the Funeral Mountains." The gold is found northeast of this place as Breyfogle hurries on to civilization and salvation.

Alvord's Gold

THE HISTORIANS CAN'T agree on the character and motives of Charles Alvord, the man who gave his name to a Mojave Desert mountain, mine, and lost mine.

Some say he was a knowledgeable prospector and respected leader; others claim that Alvord was a know-nothing Easterner who had no business in the desert. And when he did make the gold discovery in 1860 that led to the legend bearing his name, one version of the story has Alvord keeping the find to himself, in despicable violation of the basic unwritten law of prospector partnerships; the other has Alvord's partners laughing at him (they were looking for silver—the Lost Gunsight Mine—on this trip) and ignoring his find because he was a tenderfoot who knew nothing of mineral value.

But, returning from the expedition, Alvord's specimen was assayed and it proved to be of more value than anything else picked-up on the jaunt. The Alvord ore was black manganese linked with wire gold.

Writing in the June, 1950, *DESERT*, Harold Weight describes two efforts he made to find the Alvord. While much of the search for this bonanza has taken place in the south-end of Death Valley and the Owl Holes region, Weight learned of a version of the story which places the gold source in the Alvord Mountains—and he judged this account to be "far more definite in topographical details than any other I have seen."

Joe Clews had been a member of the first Alvord expedition, and only he remained in Alvord's good graces after the trip. Later, Clews accompanied Alvord on Alvord's third and last attempt to find treasure in the Mojave.

According to the version of the legend which places the mine in the Alvord Mountains, Alvord told Clews: "If you can remember where we camped when you were left on guard and Bennett (Asabel Bennett was a member of the ill-fated Death Valley '49ers) and myself went out together, you will know the place from where we started the day I found the gold. Once there I can find it again because it was in sight of a striped butte."

Alvord passed quickly from the scene (murdered, it was rumored), and for 18 years Clews tried to find Alvord's "striped butte." Finally, reports Weight, he became convinced that the campsite was Mule Spring in the Al-

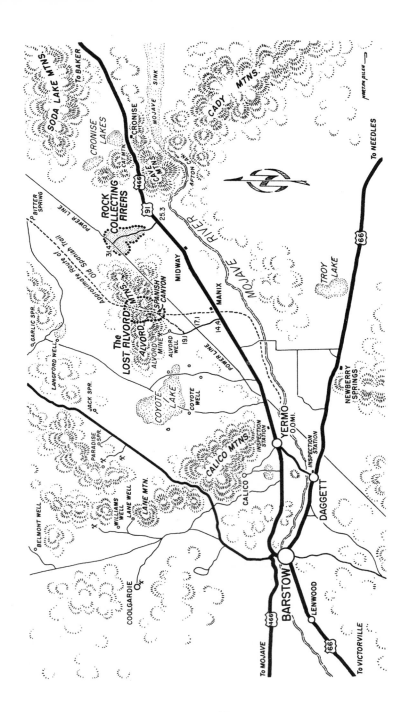

vord Mountain's Spanish (or Mule) Canyon. Once when Clews was at Mule Spring with Tom Holmes of San Bernardino, he pointed to a saddle in the hills to the southwest. "I remember watching Alvord and Bennett disappear through that saddle," he told Holmes.

The Spanish Trail (which became the Old Mormon or Salt Lake Road) passes through Spanish Canyon and there can be no doubt that Alvord and his partners passed this way more than 100 years ago. But, Mule Spring is practically impossible to find (Weight failed to locate it on two trips) because it is a wet-weather seep, not a perpetual spring.

Now look at the map accompanying this article. West and south (from a point in the middle of the canyon) is the Alvord Mine, first worked in 1855. Alvord and Bennett were seen heading southwest from Spanish Canyon.

Is it not possible that the Alvord Mine and Alvord's Lost Mine are one and the same? "No!" insist lost mine hunters. The mine's gold occurs in hematite, calcite and jasper. Alvord's gold was in manganese. Values at the mine only ran $12.75 to the ton. Alvord's sample was so rich he claims the mine could pay off the national debt (1860 level). And besides, everyone knows lost mines are never found.

Santa Rosa Gold Pockets

SOME GOLD HUNTERS are "ledge prospectors." They hike into the mountains and look for rock contacts through which run ledges of quartz. The quartz, of course, carries the gold.

Others are "placer prospectors." They sift sands and gravels for color.

But, the way to make your stake in the Santa Rosa Mountains on the south flank of California's Coachella Valley, is to become a "pocket prospector." Or so believes the dean of Pegleg searchers Henry E. W. Wilson (October, 1950, *DESERT*)

Wilson tells about three such pockets in the rugged mountains:

Pocket No. 1: In the early 1900s, Nicholas Schwartz made a strike in Rockhouse Canyon. It is said Schwartz built and occupied the rock house which gave the canyon its name. And, incidentally, Schwartz himself gave his name to a canyon in the Santa Rosas (topographical map of 1901) : "Old Nicholas Canyon."

In 1903, Wilson and John Collins prospected Rockhouse Canyon. Apparently, Nichols had by then departed the scene.

Some time later Wilson learned that Nicholas had made a strike in the area—a pocket of gold. Nicholas reportedly took out $18,000, covered up the hole, but "left more in the hole than I took out." He buried his pick and shovel in the hole to mark it.

In 1933, Wilson was back in Rockhouse Canyon. His partner was a man who had spent a year in the canyon. Wilson's partner had met a man named Pomroy, who, in turn, had known Nicholas Schwartz, thus providing the living link with the gold. The search was unsuccessful.

Pocket No. 2: In 1904, Wilson's Rockhouse Canyon partner met the cattleman Fred Clark at Clark Well, at the base of the Santa Rosas. Clark told of having nursed a rich prospector named Butler (or Buckley). The miner, knowing he was dying, told of a rich strike in the mountains which illness had forced him to leave. Wilson is convinced that this too was a pocket, for Butler had no ledge-working equipment.

Pocket No. 3: Cattleman John McCain of Julian, who owned Borrego Springs at the time, picked up a handful of likely-looking dirt one fine day

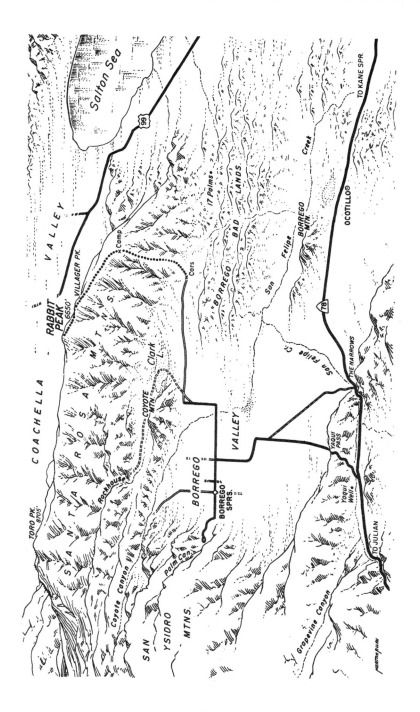

in 1893. He was in what is now known as Clark Valley (then called North Coyote Valley). The dirt payed for an assay plus a $5 profit.

Wilson panned the Clark Valley dirt twice and "got exactly nothing." Why? Because McCain's dirt contained a nugget—a piece of gold strayed from a rich Santa Rosa pocket.

There is gold all through the Santa Rosas—but abandon all prospecting savvy, forget the contacts and placer riffles—go on a nose-to-the-ground treasure hunt.

––––––––––––––

Is THERE AN INDIAN emerald mine in the Santa Rosas? Legend says such a mine was worked "from the earliest times by the desert Indians." These precious jewels flowed down the trade route to the kingdoms of central Mexico.

Marshal South (*DESERT*, December, 1948), in company with a mining engineer from Columbia, and an old Indian from Hermosillo who averred that his great grandfather had worked in the emerald mine, had some excitement looking for the treasure.

The expedition's base camp was in Rockhouse Canyon. First they looked for ". . . a ridge with rock formation on it that looks like a castle." From there they went to ". . . . *un cabeza del lobo* . . . way up . . . on top . . ."

Only the "head of the wolf" was in the bottom of a steep gully—not "way up on top." Earthquake! The landscape had been scrambled—but South and his partners found a sliver of green fire—a "small but fine emerald"— and a quantity of beryl in the jumbled rocks at their feet.

Jesuitic Treasures

ELSEWHERE IN THIS BOOK (page 220) the background of Jesuit treasure in the New World is discussed in detail.

The Jesuit Expulsion in 1767 is at the heart of all these stories. The Jesuits had *access* to silver and gold — and when Carlos III booted them out of America, it is a certainty that they took no precious metal with them.

The Jesuits say there was little or no gold-silver wealth; lost mine hunters pooh-pooh this. History, so far, is firmly joined to the Jesuit camp.

John D. Mitchell, writing in the November, 1950, *DESERT*, tells about La Purisima Concepcion Mine, "located four leagues (12 miles) south of the Tumacacori Mission."

More directions, from what Mitchell calls an "old Spanish document":

"Follow straight ahead through the pass of Los Janos to the south about three leagues from the Guadalupe mine, which is one league from the big gate of the Tumacacori mission to the south, to another gateway or pass called The Gateway to Agua Hondo (Deep Water). To the south from this pass runs a creek that empties onto the desert near the old town of Santa Cruz.

"The mine is to the east of the pass. Below the pass on the bank of the creek there are twelve arrastres and twelve patios. At the mine there is a tunnel 300 varas (835 feet) long that runs to the north. About 200 varas from the portal of this tunnel a crosscut 100 varas long leads from the main tunnel to the west. The ore in the face of this crosscut is yellow and is one-half silver and one-fifth gold. Fifty varas from the mouth of the mine in a southerly direction will be found *planchas de plata* (slabs or balls of silver) weighing from 25 to 250 pounds each. In the rock above the tunnel is the name La Purisima Concepcion, cut with a chisel. The mouth of the tunnel is covered by a copper door and fastened with a large iron lock."

There is a mass of evidence, adds Mitchell, to indicate that La Pruisima Concepcion is in the narrow pass between the west end of the Pajarita Mountains and El Ruido.

When the expulsion order came through, the Jesuits supposedly buried their wealth in the mine.

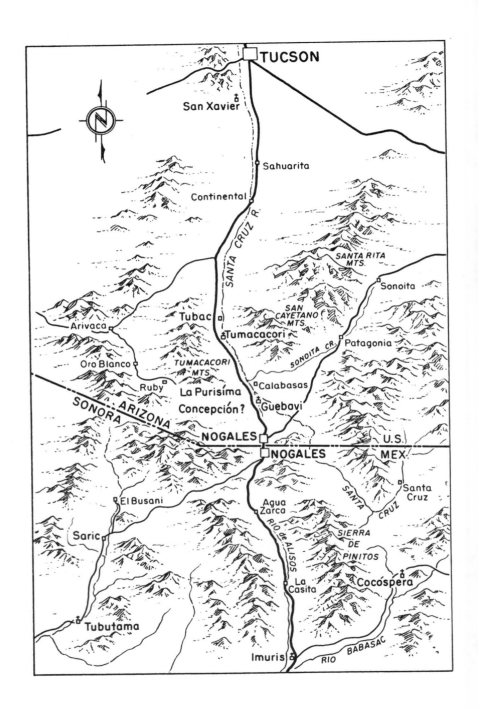

Several stories on this same theme, and in this same general area, have appeared in *DESERT* down through the years. Here is a brief recap:

Lost Guadalupe (John D. Mitchell, January, 1941). "From 1508 to 1648 the mine called the Virgin Guadalupe belonged to Tumacacori." Located one league southwest of the mission, and 1800 *varas* north of "the waters of San Ramon." Contents: "2050 mule loads of virgin silver and 905 loads of gold and silver."

Lost San Pedro (Mitchell, December, 1941). Another mine that "belonged to Tumacacori." "It measured one and one half leagues from the side of the mission to the west and when the sun rose over the lofty Santa Ritas it struck in the portal of the tunnel."

Where the Gold Lies Buried (Theron Marcos Trumbo, March, 1944). This is the golden treasure of Padre La Rue and his 18th Century colony in the Organ Mountains in southern New Mexico. Padre La Rue supposedly went into mining in a big way.

Bells of Old Guevavi (Mitchell, March, 1947). A Jesuit mission near Calabasas, a short distance northeast of Nogales, cast its own bells from "heavy black silver-copper ore which is believed to have come from the head of a rocky canyon in the southwest end of the rugged San Cayetano Mountains a short distance north of the mission." When trouble came, the padres sealed the mine and buried their treasures — including the bells.

Lost Treasure of Del Bac (Mitchell, July, 1948). Did Father Kino take silver from a rich mine which he called La Esmeralda? The silver ledge is in the mountains "about two leagues to the southwest" of Mission San Xavier Del Bac near Tucson.

Opata Silver (Mitchell, September, 1950). A mine near Mission San Cayetano de Tumacacori lies idle for 142 years until (in 1914) an old Opata Indian reworks it on a small scale. Mitchell saw five sacks of ore in 1915, and actually examined the mine in the western foothills of the San Cayetano Mountains.

Lost Escalante or *The Mine with the Iron Door* (Mitchell, July, 1952; Donald Page, October, 1956). The most famous of all Jesuit Expulsion mines. (See story on page 116).

Carreta Canyon Treasure (Mitchell, January 1953). This Jesuit cache-mine "is located somewhere along the old *Carreta* road that ran from the ancient Tumacacori Mission on the west bank of the Santa Cruz River below Tubac to Sonoyota, south of the present mining town of Ajo, Arizona."

Lost Treasure of Sonoyta (Mitchell, April, 1953). Mitchell reports on a 1917 interview with old "Dr. Juan." According to Mitchell, the Papago medicine man was past 100. Dr. Juan was raised on the Cipriano Ortega

Rancho on which the Sonoyta Mission ruins stand. The interview took place at the Quitobaquito Springs on the Arizona-Sonora border, and the subject of the conversation was the abandoned treasure of the Jesuits. Three decades later, a deer hunter reported finding an extensive — and very old — mine working "on the desert east of Fable Mountain."

Lost Bells of Tumacacori (Phyllis W. Heald, August, 1958). What happened to Tumacacori's bells described in H. M. T. Powell's *The Santa Fe Trail*, 1849-52: ". . . in the square tower there were three large bells, and there was one lying inside the church dedicated to Senor San Antonio and dated 1809." The valley floor is pock-marked with holes dug by people who had leads on the bells' whereabouts.

––––––––

WHEN GENERAL LEW WALLACE, author of *Ben Hur*, was governor of New Mexico Territory, he stated that he had seen an old Spanish document in the capitol basement that bore directly on lost treasure.

The paper told how a Christianized Indian, native of Tabira, had directed Spanish Captain deGavilan and 29 men to a golden horde in northwest Texas. The Indian had taken the white men "to a point known as Sierra de las Cenizas ("mountain of ashes") on the eastern spurs of the Guadalupes."

Ben Sublett of Monahan is said to have made frequent trips into the Guadalupes—and he never seemed to lack for gold. Sublett died in 1892. His son, Ross, a resident of Carlsbad, "claims to have a distinct recollection of his dad taking him to the mine when he was a small boy."

DESERT'S story (March, 1948) is by John D. Mitchell.

Pedro's Gold Dust

In 1938 A Mexican peddled a flask of gold dust (actually small grain-sized nuggets) to Dr. J. E. Stains of Delta, Utah. Happy to have an outlet for his gold, the Mexican brought 20 pounds of the same placer gold to Dr. Stains. One can imagine the sort of stir this caused in Millard County, which is definitely not gold country.

The Mexican, a sheepherder, disappeared from the scene. Inquiry revealed that he had done most of his sheep-tending in the House Mountains, 50 miles west of Delta.

A stockman remembered the Mexican—and also recalled seeing a "treasure map" in his possession. The map, recalled the stockman, was very old.

There was only one place in the county that had a gold history—North Canyon near Marjum Pass. The gravels here were well known, certainly not "lost," but they were far from being spectacular producers. Pedro had been seen in North Canyon with his sheep, so two prospectors made another search of the area and found a cache of old Spanish hand tools.

The parts were beginning to fall into place, but the most important part—the actual site where the Mexican sheepherder had struck it rich—was and is missing.

DESERT's story (April, 1951) is by Frank Beckwith.

———————————

John D. Mitchell (*DESERT*, February, 1949) tells about another lost Utah placer. To be more specific (but not much more) Mitchell places the "Pothole Placers" in the land of the Snake Indians—"at the base of a low-lying granite mountain." Atop the "iron-stained mesas" were potholes filled with standing rainwater.

The potholes were also pots-of-gold for two prospectors. It was in these rock depressions, says Mitchell, that they found $100,000 in nuggets.

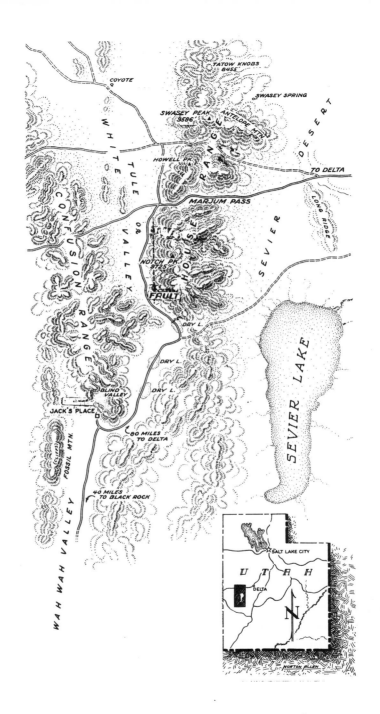

COYOTE

TATOW KNOBS
8455

SWASEY SPRING

SWASEY PEAK
9586

ANTELOPE MTN.

HOWELL PK.

W H I T E

T U L E   OR

V A L L E Y

C O N F U S I O N   R A N G E

MARJUM PASS

NOTCH PK.
9725

FAULT

H O U S E   R A N G E

R A N G E

D E S E R T

TO DELTA

S E V I E R

LONG RIDGE

DRY L.

DRY L.

BLIND
VALLEY

JACK'S PLACE

DRY L.

60 MILES
TO DELTA

40 MILES
TO BLACK ROCK

W A H   W A H   V A L L E Y

FOSSIL MTN.

(CLIFFS)

S E V I E R   L A K E

SALT LAKE CITY

U T A H

DELTA

N

NORTON ALLEN

— 100 —

Loma Gold

KARL HUDSON KNEW a Spanish-American from New Mexico named Pedro Giron. Giron, in turn, is believed to be the last man alive to have known and talked to a member of the gold party that made the big strike in the Animas River Valley of southern Colorado. Hudson told the story in the July, 1951, *DESERT*.

The man Giron talked to was a French-Canadian known only as Pierre. Giron had met Pierre when the latter was old and broken.

But in the mid-1880s, Pierre was young and full of fire. He had organized a party of 28 horsemen from northern New Mexico villages to follow him into the Las Animas Valley. He had a sample of rich gold picked-up on his trek south to Santa Fe. There was enough where that came from to make every one of the 28 men rich for life.

Pierre had not exaggerated. The men quickly found the ledge, built a crude arrastre, and recovered gold that entire summer.

At the first snowfall they left their camp—and ran into Utes. Actually, the Utes had been waiting for weeks to bushwhack the party. The Indians had learned from other tribesmen in the Southwest what happened to a land and its people when the whiteman found the yellow metal.

The white party had time to bury most of its gold, and scatter—every man for himself—when the Utes struck. Pierre and Juan Sanchez were the only ones to make it out alive, or more accurately, half-alive. Wrote Hudson: "All desire for adventure was gone"—and understandably so. Neither Pierre nor Juan returned to the Animas.

The clues: wide valley, hot springs and red cliffs. Only the Animas supplies these features in this country.

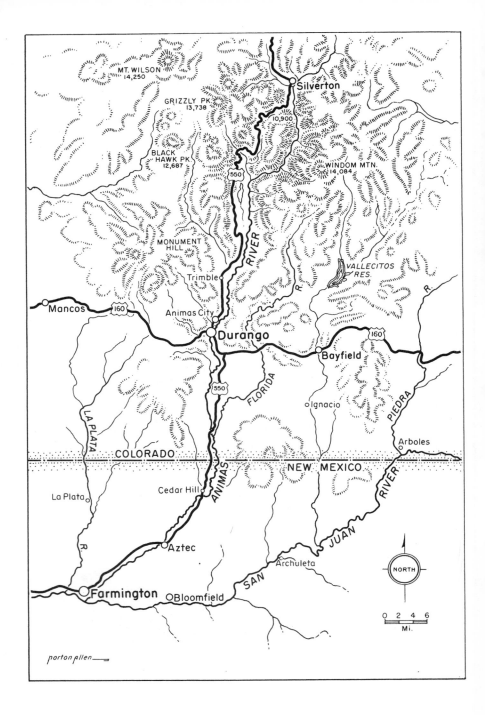

Irish Cavalier

PATRICK O'DONOHUE — in Spanish, *Don Padriac Odonoju* — was an Irish "warrior" who had given the English some bad moments in the mid-1700s. So well did he do his work, the King of Spain adopted him, gave him a name change, and sent him off to the northern frontier of Mexico to see what he could do about taming the desert and its Apache denizens. Apparently, Odonoju did a credible job, and the Spanish king "rewarded" the Irishman by giving him the deed to "12 leagues in the Land of Papagueria." This was still farther north, still deeper in the country being troubled by the Apaches (the Papagos, for whom the land was named, were friendly), and still deeper in the desert. The story is told in the September, 1951, *DESERT*, by L. James Rasmussen.

It was a "hellish grant," but Odonoju liked it and he stayed on. Indeed, he built quite a hacienda, and mission. This land he called "Garden of Solitude," the mission was dedicated to "the four Evangelists." The whole lay in the Altar Valley.

Rasmussen says this fairy tale ended on 1780. "The arm of tragedy swung down on Don Padriac's Garden of Solitude." The Apaches killed the lot. "That which could not be destroyed by blows was leveled by flame."

Neither blows nor flame can destroy gold—and gold is what Don Padriac had used to ornament the *Mission de los Quatros Evangelistas* . . . gold that had been brought to the rancho by Papagos mining secret places in the surrounding country. The Apaches, apparently, had not as yet learned the value of gold. They killed, broke and burned, taking weapons and implements and other useful items, including trinkets and doodads. Gold bars were too heavy, too useless.

"Nothing survived . . . the beautiful garden that had once bloomed in a desert died." The blowing sands covered the Irish Cavalier's golden church.

Surely Rasmussen wrote this yarn with tongue-in-cheek. To lose a trinket or even a bell from a church is understandable—but to lose a whole church-rancho ignores the fact that civilization, as we know it, was transplanted to Mexico long before the Pilgrims stepped ashore on Plymouth

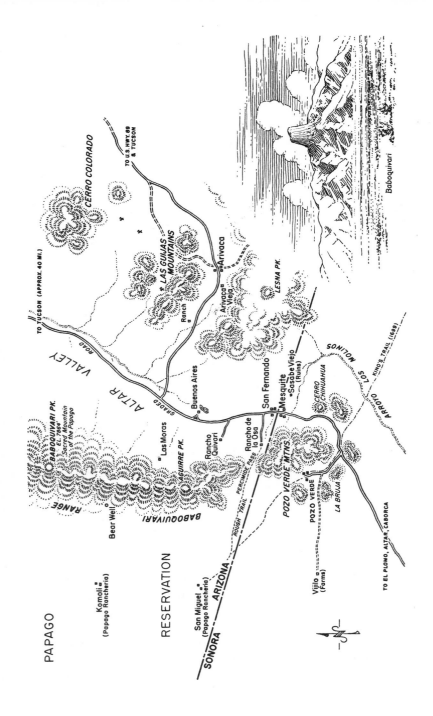

Baboquivari

Rock, and that Mexican civilization had its officials, civil servants and records-in-triplicate the moment Cortez landed on Mexican shores.

Elsewhere in this book (page 220) the wealth of the Sonoran frontiersmen is disputed.

Still, if you happen to be in the Altar Valley and you stumble across a charred beam—dig!

Ruins of Jesuit Church in Sinaloa.

Monterrey Loot

WHEN AN ANGLO border bandit killed or robbed, he headed for Mexico and safety — or so we have been led to believe by countless Old West stories.

The Mexican murderer-thief (more often referred to as a "smuggler") did the same thing in reverse — that is, he traveled north to the U. S. and safety.

In 1881, a large group of Mexican "smugglers," fresh from plundering banks and the cathedral in Monterrey, were making their way north to the vicinity of Skeleton Canyon in the Peloncillo Mountains along the Arizona-New Mexico line. According to one source, they had a cigar box filled with diamonds valued at a million dollars; 39 bars of gold worth $600,000; $90,000 in silver coin; and gold statuary figures and stacks of gold coin.

Hidden in the rocks was a gang of cut-throats headed by one Jim Hughes, lieutenant to the notorious "Curly Bill" Brocius.

Hughes was about to perpetrate a two-way double-cross. First, he was going to kill and rob the Mexicans (which he did) —a group he had befriended earlier in Sonora (and had thus been able to learn their time schedule for entering the U.S.). Secondly, Hughes was going to keep the loot to himself, cutting-out his boss, Curly Bill.

The ambush, having come off to perfection, the boys set off to stop the stampeding pack of mules laden with treasure. They accomplished this with rifle fire. But, this caused an unforeseen problem: the Hughes bunch had no pack animals to tote their ill-won and heavy spoils.

So, the boys filled their pockets and — one account says they dumped the surplus wealth into an old shaft — buried the remaining treasure under several feet of dirt.

Hughes now returned to his headquarters at Gayleyville to pretend nothing was new to Curly Bill. He left two men, Zwing Hunt and Billy Grounds, with orders to move the loot to a predetermined and more advantageous site.

Hunt and Grounds hired a Mexican teamster and his outfit, and the trio relocated the treasure. The poor Mexican, of course, was paid off with a few direct rounds of ammunition, and Hunt and Grounds headed for a

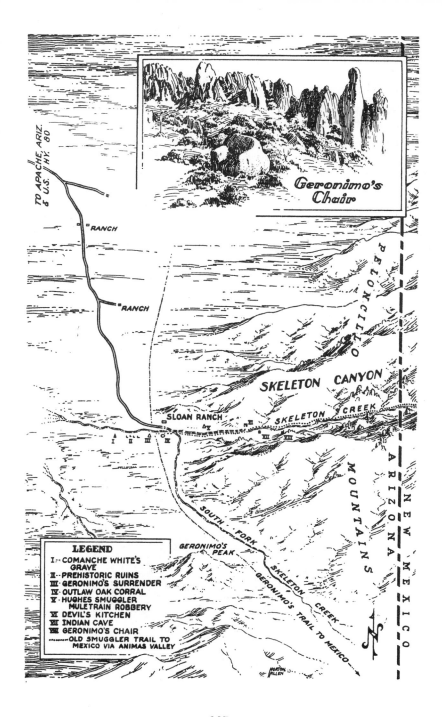

Geronimo's Chair

TO APACHE, ARIZ.
& U.S. HY. 80

"RANCH

"RANCH

PELONCILLO

SKELETON CANYON

SLOAN RANCH   SKELETON   CREEK

SOUTH   FORK

GERONIMO'S
PEAK

SKELETON CREEK

GERONIMO'S TRAIL TO MEXICO

MOUNTAINS

ARIZONA

NEW MEXICO

LEGEND
I -- COMANCHE WHITE'S
      GRAVE
II -- PREHISTORIC RUINS
III -- GERONIMO'S SURRENDER
IV -- OUTLAW OAK CORRAL
V -- HUGHES SMUGGLER
      MULETRAIN ROBBERY
VI -- DEVIL'S KITCHEN
VII -- INDIAN CAVE
VIII -- GERONIMO'S CHAIR
......OLD SMUGGLER TRAIL TO
      MEXICO VIA ANIMAS VALLEY

MORTON
ALLEN

glorious drunk at the Stockton Ranch. (In the July, 1940, *DESERT*, John D. Mitchell says the treasure was relocated north "two days from Skeleton Canyon, a distance estimated between 40 and 50 miles.")

These were flinty times. Grounds was killed and Hunt severely wounded in a brawl that grew out of their post-reburial celebration.

Hunt, recovering, set out to double-cross his boss, Hughes, by hiding out from him. But, soon gangrene set in, and, dying, he drew a map to the loot burial site. True to his stripe, he gave the map to his uncle, not to Hughes.

The dying man pinpointed the cache with an accuracy that should be the envy of every lost treasure burier: "at the foot of Davis Mountain," quoting from the story in the November, 1951, *DESERT*, by Weldon Heald, "to the east stretch open, rolling plains and from the summit of the peak you

can see a good-sized slice of New Mexico. A mile and a half west curves a canyon hemmed in on the far side by wooded hills, while the east wall is formed by a sheer rock precipice. Through this canyon comes a stream which flows over a ledge in a 10-foot cascade. Hunt said he and Billy Grounds took a bath under the waterfall after they had buried the treasure. He put down on the map, also, the location of two springs about a mile and a quarter apart, and called the northerly one Silver Spring and the other, Gum Spring. Then he carefully described how to find the exact spot where the loot was buried. It was between the two springs, but a little nearer Silver. The place was marked by a square-sided stone, one foot thick and three feet high, and on the east face of the stone Hunt chiseled two crosses, one above the other. Walk 20 paces east, he said, and you are standing on top of the buried treasure of the Chiricahuas."

Hunt's directions are explicit, and no one who knows his way around the backcountry could miss becoming wealthy — except for one thing:

There is no "Davis Mountain" in this country!

Gold coins, probably scattered from the fleeing pack mules, have been picked up in Skeleton Canyon.

And in 1921, according to an interview in the August, 1941, *DESERT*, Ross Sloan of the Sloan Ranch at the mouth of Skeleton Canyon, reported that ". . . an old pale-looking fellow with a long white beard drove up with a sorry-looking team — a gray mule and a poor white horse. A little boy was in the wagon with him. The man wanted to know if this was Skeleton Canyon, and I said it was . . . next day one of our sons went up to see where the outfit was camped. But they were gone. You could see where a large box had been taken out from under a big rock. Years later, Sam Olney told me about an old man coming to his smelter with some silver bars for treatment. The fellow told him he got them from Skeleton Canyon."

ANOTHER STORY in the buried loot category concerns itself with Emperor Maximilian's riches. When ill-fated Maximilian saw his Mexican empire was doomed, he loaded his treasure into 15 *carretas* and sent it north in the direction of Texas.

Unfortunately the caravan met six lean and hungry Missourians, ex-Confederate soldiers, out to make — or take — their fortune.

The slaughter took place at Castle Gap, 15 miles east of Horse Head Crossing on the Pecos River.

John Mitchell, writing in the April, 1948, *DESERT*, says the Missouri lads buried that part of the treasure which they were not able to stuff in their saddle bags. Illness and bullets wiped out the bandits within a short time after the highjack.

Shotgun Mine

GOLD IS WHERE YOU find it — and so are clues to lost mines. Gus Wirt found his waybill in an old tin chest found in an El Dorado, California, house which he and his uncle were remodeling.

Writing in the January, 1952, *DESERT*, Wirt discloses: "From the letters, we gathered that L. O. Long and John Carthright during the 1860s worked placer ground along the Consumes River south and west of El Dorado. John Carthright had moved to Fresno in 1871 and the letters were an account of the travels and prospecting of his former partner. References were made to the 'Palms,' 'Dale' and the 'Sheep Mountains.' We translated these as Twentynine Palms, the old Dale mining district east of there and the Sheep Hole Mountains."

The Sheep Holes are a short, north-west trending range extremely short of water sources (the "holes" refer, no doubt, to natural cisterns in the rock which sheep drank from—but rain is a stranger to this area and it is doubtful these "tanks" are wet more than a couple of months out of the year). There is only one reliable water source in the range—the spring at the Sheep Hole Mine on the extreme end of the mountain at the pass above Dale Dry Lake.

I quote again from Wirt's account of what he found in the letters:

"The last letter was dated June, 1873, and was posted in San Bernardino. It wasn't the same handwriting nor did it use the same type of expression as did Long's previous communications.

"Long evidently was not very well educated, and his own letters were rather difficult to read. This last one . . . was well-written . . . probably dictated by Long to some doctor or friend in San Bernardino.

"In it Long revealed that he had brought out a total of 100 ounces of gold from his workings and planned to return as soon as he was well enough to travel."

On his last journey into the desert, he had fallen, hurting his leg. So painful was the injury that Long found it difficult to carry his shotgun—so he cached it near his diggings. Long never returned to the Sheep Holes, for he died soon after. Wirt found a letter from the marshall at San Bernardino,

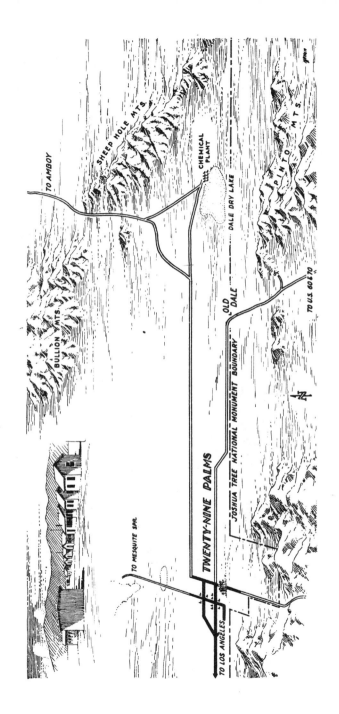

dated June 22, 1873, and addressed to Carthright, asking whether Long's partner would arrange for the burial.

In one of Long's letters to Carthright, Wirt gathered this information: the placer deposit was in a "brush canyon about 15 miles almost due east of the salt lake" (Dale Dry Lake).

Long had dug and walled-up a shallow spring at his mine. The diggings were "around the bend" and "just below the spring."

Phil Sullivan, an old miner in Twentynine Palms, told Wirt that in 1925 he had found a fine English shotgun and several shells under a rock ledge in the Sheep Holes.

He picked-up the shotgun "at a place east of Dale Dry Lake back in the hills 10 miles or so" but "couldn't remember ever having seen a spring in those hills."

Goler's Gold

GOLER (NO ONE REMEMBERS his given name) was in the Red Rock Canyon country north of Mojave in 1867—traveling alone and afoot from Death Valley to Los Angeles.

Apparently he was prospecting along the way, which means he was keeping off the established trails.

Pausing to drink at a spring, he saw a sizable gold nugget. He scooped several more from the water, made a quick survey of the canyon, and proceeded on his way—this time with a much lighter step.

Goler knew he had struck it rich—and he knew it would take considerable capital to exploit a placer mine so far from the nearest town and civilization.

Pausing on the top of a little hill near the east side of the valley, the German prospector "planted" his Spencer Repeating Rifle in the ground. It would be his beacon, guiding him back to his fortune-maker.

In Los Angeles, Goler had some trouble convincing men-with-money that his mine was worth their risk. The nuggets were impressive, but the desert was big and hot and hard to milk. One man—Grant Price Cuddeback—listened. An occasional miner and full-time rancher, Cuddeback made three tries at finding Goler's placer, with no luck—or rather, with only partial luck. On their last safari, Goler and Cuddeback made a strike in Red Rock Canyon, which they worked for several years.

From this point on, our story becomes a little muddy. Some say Goler disappeared from the Mojave Desert; others that he continued as a familiar figure. Indeed, writing in the March, 1952, *DESERT*, Ada Giddings quotes the late Finley Buhn of Goler Heights as saying Buhn's uncle "Slate Range Jack" Kurlitz (the correct spelling is *Kuhrts*) saw Goler on many of his freighting hauls, *and that Goler returned to his golden canyon—appearing on present-day maps as "Goler Canyon"—and successfully worked the placers!*

Whether it was Goler or someone else who took the gold out of Goler Canyon, the fact is the place was mined—and it is a good bet that Goler Canyon is the bonanza Cuddeback and Goler went searching for.

Finley Buhn told author Giddings that on one occasion, Uncle Slate

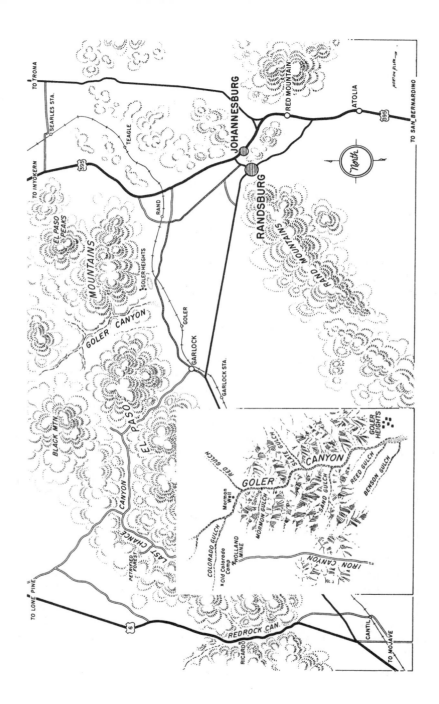

Range Jack asked Goler where he had found a certain nugget. Goler pointed to the large canyon which today bears his name.

And here is more proof: In 1917, Goler's gun was found by the Munseys—widowed mother and son—of the Lazy-M Ranch near the mouth of Red Rock Canyon. Ada Giddings, who with her husband had homesteaded on the Mojave, were neighbors of the Munseys.' Mrs. Giddings recalls the excitement caused by the Goler gun find.

Ed Maginnis (who later became a judge at Randsburg) was a Wells Fargo agent at Garlock (now a ghost town). He estimated that more than a million dollars was taken out of the Goler mining district.

Thus, in Goler's story, we have a unique twist—a lost mine which was rediscovered—at least it would seem so.

The Lost Escalante

ONE OF THE MOST famous of all Southwest lost mines — the one with the iron door—has intrigued many serious students of Southwest history and legend. The John D. Mitchell account was part of the July, 1952, *DESERT*. Donald Page also contributed an article on this subject (October, 1956).

The mine is actually the Lost Escalante, subject of Harold Bell Wright's book, "The Mine With the Iron Door." The story is that the Jesuits worked the Escalante in the Santa Catalina Mountains near Tucson, prior to their expulsion, in 1767, from Spanish territory.

A large number of friendly Papago Indians were employed in building a hiding place for the highgrade ore which, of course, the Jesuits would not be able to take with them. But, they had every intention of returning to the New World, with its rich treasures of heathen souls to be converted and gold to be separated from its matrix.

Mitchell writes that "the treasure vault was near the south bank of the Canada del Oro . . . the ruins of the old camp and the foundations of the little chapel where the priests said mass may still be seen." The iron door seals the treasure chamber.

On San Juan's Day in June, 1796, Apaches raided the mine camp, killing and scattering the Papagos. The settlement was destroyed and forgotten.

Mitchell says a clue to the Escalante is a *ventana*—a natural hole in the rock resembling a window. The mine is "one league northwest of the *ventana*."

Donald Page reports that the first known record of gold discovery in the Canada Del Oro was on June 29, 1843—long after the Jesuit business. A Colonel Antonio Narbona, commanding a strong military expedition against the Apaches, camped here and found placer nuggets.

The years that followed saw much Apache trouble in Arizona, but by May, 1870, "most of the men and boys of Tucson were hard at work at the same spot, each panning between $12 and $30 a day."

The Apaches once again scattered the miners, chasing them out of the Santa Catalinas for a 10-year period.

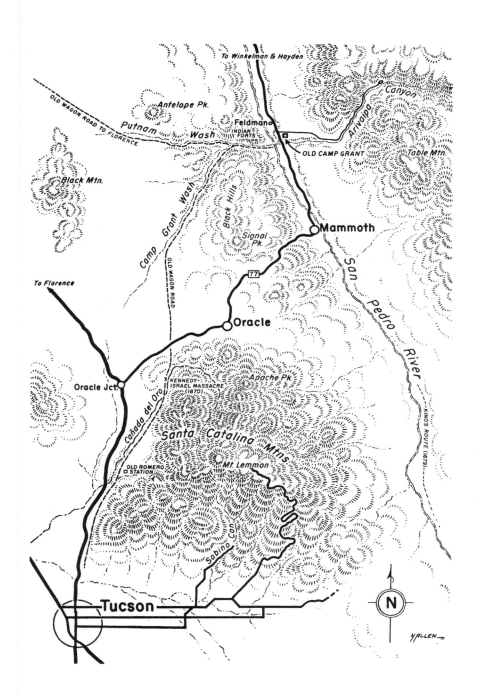

The *gringos* became active in these mountains starting in 1880. The *Americanos* brought with them the legends and fables about rich mines which they had gathered from Mexicans in dusty Sonora villages. The placers were fine—but somewhere in the Catalinas there was a real treasure aging behind an iron door.

————————

IN THIS SAME general area is set the story of the Lost Yuma Ledge (John D. Mitchell, *DESERT*, April, 1941)—the "Yuma" here being the nickname of an ex-Army officer, courtmartialed for his amazing bookkeeping abilities while serving as quartermaster at the Yuma post.

Friendly Apache Indians (being an embezzler no doubt helped Yuma in his relations with the redskins) lead our hero to a rich outcropping of "rose quartz rich in coarse gold." All this on ". . . a ridge between the San Pedro River on the east and a deep rocky canyon which terminated a short distance to the west of where they were standing." But, Yuma did not last too long after that. The Apaches were not friendly for too long at a time.

Vampire Bat Gold

IN THE LATE 1800s there was considerable placer mining in the Arivaca, Arizona, environs—which is Papago country.

At the little store the boys would barter nuggets for the necessities of life. No one thought much about one of the regular customers—an old Indian—who brought in his share of gold, but was never seen to work a claim.

When the placers gave out, the miners drifted off—all except the old Papago, who continued to bring in nuggets whenever his family needed supplies. Indeed, he was quite a familiar sight at the Tucson Fiestas—a rich Indian! But where did his wealth come from?

He was followed wherever he went—but there were only three contact points in his life; the store, his brush hut in the Baboquivari Mountains, and the Tucson Fiesta. None is a potential candidate for a gold stampede.

John D. Mitchell (*DESERT*, August, 1952) gives the answer:

"Many years ago while trailing a wounded deer across the foothills on the eastern slopes of the Baboquivari Mountains," the Papago revealed to the Arivaca storekeeper, "I sat down to rest on the top of a long ridge running in a northerly direction from the peak . . . "

Just then he saw a flight of large vampire bats emerging from a crevice—a mine stope! The Papago investigated, and found an abandoned Spanish cache—buckskin bags full of gold nuggets. There were gold bars, too, and mine tools and a shrine.

The Indian, frightened at intruding on the eerie workings of departed souls, hastened away from the taboo cave. But, he was not so apprehensive that he could not allow himself to take just one bag of nuggets.

This he buried under the floor of his hut.

The merchant, elated over the information windfall, spent the night preparing for a trek into the Baboquivaris. Next morning he was greeted at his door by the Indian who had had second thoughts about telling a secret to a paleface.

"I waited until all the bats were back in the hole," he said, "then I closed the entrance with rocks and earth."

"No more bats. They all will die in the hole, and no white man will ever find the mine."

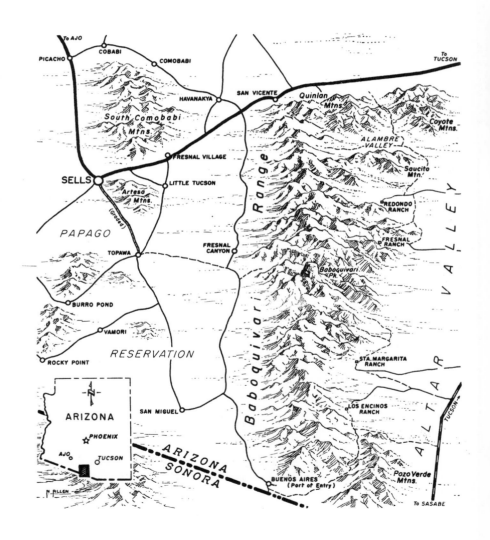

Lead of Santa Clara

GEORGE GARDNER, WRITING in the September, 1952, *DESERT,* quotes an anonymous "old cattleman turned prospector" throughout his story of the lost lead-silver ledge on the Santa Clara River.

The mine is in the area where the river is crossed by the Old Spanish Trail (and, incidentally, Highway 91).

The lead ledge was discovered by one Jim Houdon who was with a wagon train bound for California in 1852. One of the wagons bumped over the ledge, exposing it to Houdon's gaze. He returned to Utah some years later and walked right up to the riverside treasure.

He took out two good loads, but was frightened off by an approaching wagon. Houdon tried to cover up the diggings by flooding the shaft before scampering off.

Exit Houdon, enter Robert Lloyd on the wagon, heading for Pine Valley.

Lloyd saw Houdon leaving, so he investigated and found the ledge. But Lloyd took only enough ore for an assay.

When the report came in, Lloyd knew he was within a hair's breadth of being a rich man.

But the Santa Clara had an ace up its sleeve: a cloudburst flood wiped out riverbank landmarks.

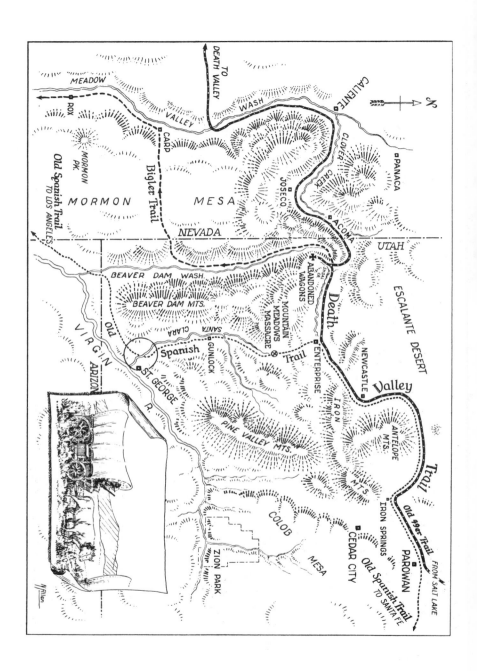

TO DEATH VALLEY

MEADOW VALLEY WASH

CALIENTE

ROX

CARP

MORMON PK.

Old Spanish Trail TO LOS ANGELES

MORMON MESA

Bigler Trail

NEVADA

CLOVER CREEK

JOSECO

PANACA

ACOMA

UTAH

BEAVER DAM WASH

BEAVER DAM MTS.

1857 ABANDONED WAGONS

ESCALANTE DESERT

MOUNTAIN MEADOWS MASSACRE

Death

VIRGIN

Old Spanish

SANTA CLARA

GUNLOCK

ST. GEORGE

R.

ARIZONA

ENTERPRISE

NEWCASTLE

Trail

PINE VALLEY MTS.

IRON MTS.

Valley

ANTELOPE MTS.

Old 49er Trail FROM SALT LAKE

PAROWAN

IRON SPRINGS

Trail

COLOB MESA

ZION PARK

CEDAR CITY

Old Spanish Trail TO SANTA FE

N/Allen

— 122 —

Pima Gold

INSTEAD OF HAVING to spend old age as a saloon derelict, gaining his booze by telling and retelling the one story he knew so well — the story of how he had been cheated out of a fortune by fate—the old prospector might have had enough gold to buy every saloon in Arizona.

He came close. If only he had known what John D. Mitchell (writing in the October '52 *DESERT*) and every other Western writer knows: "Indians, traveling on foot or horseback, often follow a straight course."

The Indians in question here were a small band of Pimas. "Some years ago" they had guided a party of bear hunters into the Ord Mountains, 50 miles northeast of Phoenix. Returning (in a straight line) from the north base of Mt. Ord to the northern foothills of the Superstition Mountains, the Pimas stumbled across the bleached bones of two white men. Near their remains was a mound of "milky white quartz generously flecked with free gold."

The Pima guides later showed the pretty rocks to our newly-arrived prospector friend who knew so little about Indians' travel habits.

The poor man backtracked the Pimas' trail—but his only "reward" was an old age filled with frustration and despair.

The skeletons, Mitchell believes, belonged to a couple of troopers from Fort McDowell who had made the original strike while deer hunting, but later lost their lives during a different kind of hunt—Apaches hunting anything on two legs that invaded what they considered to be their sacred corner of the earth.

————————

A JOHN D. MITCHELL story ("Don Joaquin and His Gold Mine") in the May, 1943, *DESERT*, has 50 bars of gold and 30 bags of gold nuggets cached in a cave near Montezuma's Head in the Estrella Mountains south of Phoenix.

Pima and Maricopa Indian legends tell of ancestors working this mine for a Spaniard, Don Joaquin Campoy.

Santa Catarina Silver

"WHEN THE SUN shines directly through the east portal of the mission courtyard, then the silver mine of the Dominican padres will be found on the sidewall of a narrow canyon directly beneath where the sun rests in the sky, about six leagues from the mission."

This is the chief clue to the lost silver mine near Baja California's Mission Santa Catarina Martyr. This mission was established in 1797 by the Dominican fathers. All that remains of the structure today is a low ridge of adobe.

Randall Henderson wrote the lost mine story for the November, 1952, *DESERT*. His information came from Eugene Albanes, a 70-year-old Diegueno Indian who had married a Pai Pai woman. The directive to the mine was handed down in the idiom of the Pai Pai. Albanes translated it to Spanish, and Arles Adams, Henderson's perennial Baja California traveling companion, converted it into English.

Albanes told of the time a Mexican boy herding cows caught sight of a mine entrance. He investigated and found the opening closed with thick timbers.

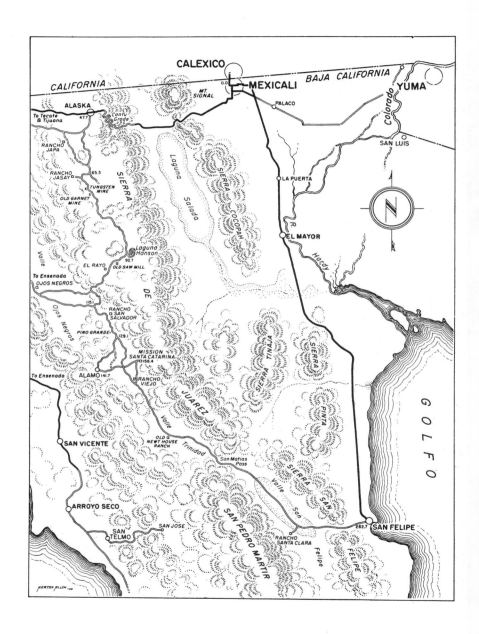

Waterfall Gold

A LETTER DATED MAY 28, 1904, fell into the hands of a prospector known as "Long Tom" Watson, and a Grand Canyon lost treasure was born. Long Tom found the letter six years after it was written.

"Dear Brother," it read, ". . . I had found ground covered with gold nuggets in the canyon and had collected an ore sack full of them preparatory to coming out. That night, two I had suspected of following me rode into camp."

The writer threw the sack of nuggets into the mouth of a small cave under a 22-foot waterfall. If the two strangers were friendly, the gold could easily be recovered; if they had other designs, then they would leave the canyon empty-handed.

They had other designs, and in the fight that ensued, the letter writer was severely wounded, dying a short time afterwards—but not before he had written the letter—and drawn a treasure map.

By June, 1914, the discouraged prospector decided to call it quits. On his way out of the Canyon, on the Tanner Trail, he "heard the sound of distant water. It came not from the river, but from the south . . . an unexpected waterfall about 700 feet up the wall of the gorge."

This was it! He stuffed his pockets with the biggest nuggets, but while leaping from the lip of the cave, he slipped and went over the side with the water. His leg was broken below the knee.

It's one thing to be a down-and-out prospector sitting in Grand Canyon with a broken leg; it's quite another proposition to be a wealthy prospector in the same circumstance.

Long Tom gritted his teeth and dragged his body to his burros down on the trail. His next stop was the Martin Buggelin Rancho on the South Rim.

After a long stay in the hospital, Long Tom returned to the Canyon—but he was not able to find the vagrant waterfall. There is no permanent waterfall to the west of Tanner Trail. There can be no doubt that when

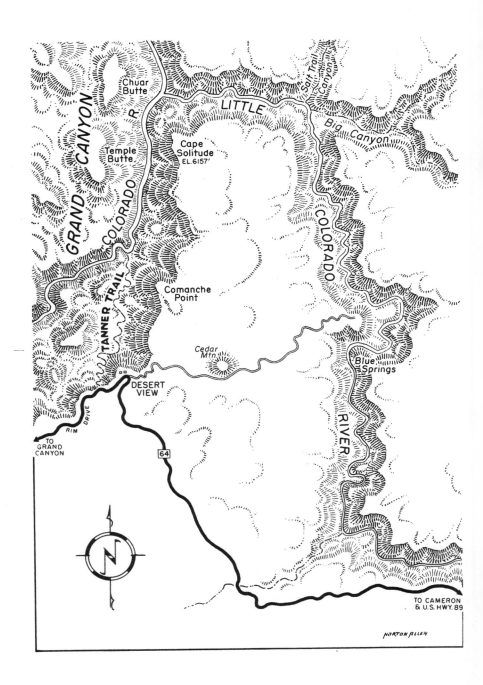

water does flow over the rock walls here, it is immediately after a heavy rainfall—and heavy rainfalls have a way of creating new channels, filling caves with debris and just generally raising hell with the landscape.

Gladwell Richardson wrote the story in *DESERT* (March, 1953).

————————

THE "CANYON WILDERNESS" of northern Arizona is the setting for the "Lost Mine of Coconino," whose history is related by Gladwell Richardson in the July, 1950, *DESERT*. (Sometimes it is called "Lost City of Coconino County" because there were quite a few buildings at the gold workings.)

One of the men who reportedly stumbled across the mine was a Flagstaff character known as "Bearhunter" Howard.

The Blond Mayo

PERHAPS SOMEDAY THE television screens will be full of Juan Morales, a blond Mayo Indian from Sonora. And perhaps American small fry will be joining "Blond Mayo" clubs, and at Christmas time they'll get genuine and official Blond Mayo sharp-shooter air rifles and Blond Mayo lost mine hats.

Picture a steel-nerved light-haired Indian riding alone into Apache country to his secret mine in the Cerro Colorado Mountains on the east flank of Arizona's Altar Valley. Our Indian hero pauses to scan the skyline. Something moves. It is too small for normal human vision to make-out. But Juan Morales smiles, lifts his rifle to his shoulder, and shoots. Hundreds of yards away, the Apache warrior, who only days before had cut-down Juan's friend, is himself dispatched.

The blond Indian continues to his treasure-house from which he extracts another six mule-loads of " . . . quartz . . . matted together with wires and masses of bright yellow gold . . . (with) a blue indigo tinge, probably bromide of silver." The quote is from John D. Mitchell's story in the May, 1953, *DESERT*. Juan ". . . was gaunt, eagle-eyed, tireless and remorseless as doom when it came to avenging the death of a friend . . ."

The Blond Mayo made his headquarters in Arivaca. His partner was his brother, Fermin. Mitchell hints that his information for this story came from two men who knew the Blond Mayo, Don Manuel Gonzales and Don Teofilio Ortiz, both of Arivaca.

It is believed by some that the Morales brothers came north to Arivaca for the sole and express purpose of mining the chimney (or pipe) of gold in the Cerro Colorados under the natural rock formation "carved by wind and sand to resemble the body of a woman lying outstretched on top of the highest ridge." This stone mass is known as the Black Princess.

The Blond Mayo died "when old and full of years." Fermin passed on in the 1930s, and is buried at Arivaca. With them lies the secret of the mine that made them wealthy.

Was it the fabled Sopori Mine discovered and worked by the early Spaniards?

Old maps place the Sopori in the shadow of the Black Princess.

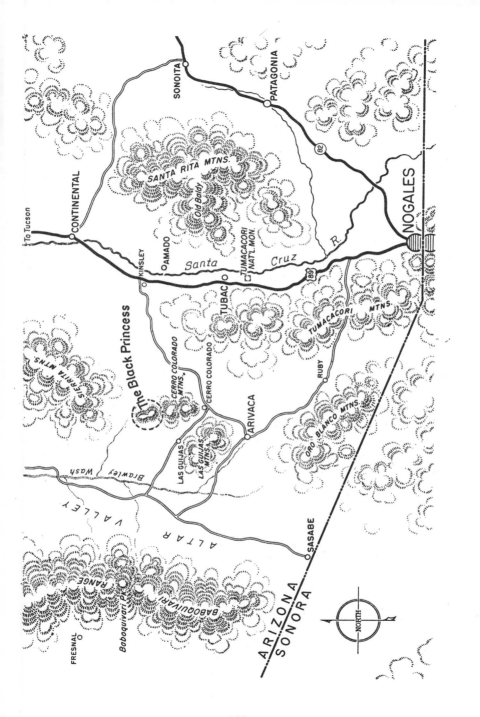

Sierra Sombrera

DURING THE FIRST World War, tungsten was king. Prospectors knew that a good tungsten mine could make a man a good living.

"Cap" Linger of Ajo, Arizona, was such a prospector. He worked north from Ajo with his nose to the ground, looking for tungsten. Through the Batamote Hills and the Sauceda Mountains he walked in a painstaking search that took weeks and months.

The big strike came in the Sierra Sombrera (now known by its English name, Hat Mountain) north of the Saucedas.

But Cap was not destined to die a rich man. Happily (for everyone else on earth) the war came to an end and tungsten joined the likes of sand and gravel in the prospector's scheme of things.

Cap and his wife struggled with the mine a short time, then went East. There Cap died, and years later his wife returned to Ajo.

And then — World War II, and once again tungsten see-sawed into the blue. But, where was Cap's diggings? Even with the map he had drawn, there was no finding the mine.

At the time *DESERT* published the Sierra Sombrera story by Kenneth E. Hickok in the June, 1953, issue, Cap's friends were still prowling the maze of canyons at the foot of Hat Mountain.

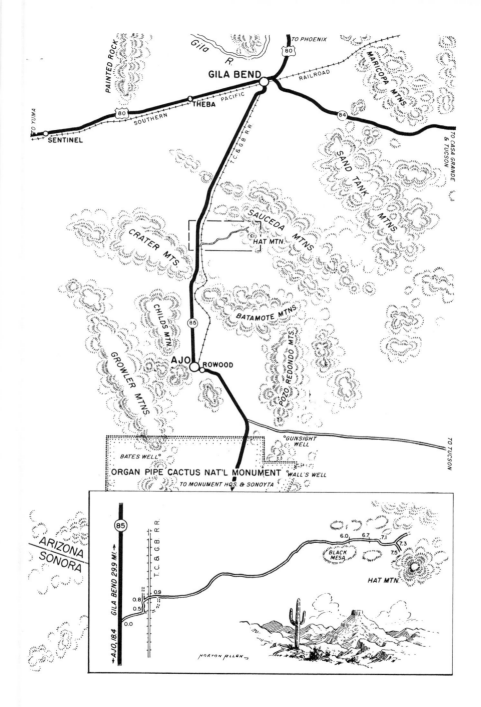

Blue Bucket Gold

THE YEAR WAS 1845. The wagon train was bound for Oregon. At gravelly Ford Crossing on the Humboldt River, the group split into two parties, one continuing along the Humboldt, the other striking due north into the Black Rock country.

This latter group passed the Black Rock Mountains and climbed to the top of the next rise.

From this vantage, the pioneers "could see the Twin Sister Peaks." Camp was made at a spring in the canyon below—and it was here that some of the people picked-up "pretty yellow rocks." In fact, the kiddies filled several blue buckets with the pebbles.

Then a member of the party passed away and her grave was marked with one of the blue buckets.

While crossing the Deschutes River several of the wagons capsized and most of the yellow rocks were lost.

Some time later, when it was learned just what the pretty rocks were made of, the gold rush was on. A party of 90 persons made a try for the treasure, but were turned back by Indians.

In 1879, a California prospector learned from the agent at the Malheur Indian Reservation that he had found a grave by a spring about three miles from the agency. At the same place were heavy timbers like those used to brake wagons on a steep incline. There was also a wide track down the mountain.

John D. Mitchell's story was in the August, 1953, *DESERT*.

————————

HUMBOLDT—NOW A GHOST TOWN — is where L. W. Morgan's "Lost Lead-Silver Mine in Nevada" (*DESERT*, April, 1949) lies waiting discovery. Morgan wrote that in 1910 he met the young men who gave birth to this tale, and "I believe the story they told is absolutely true."

The boys had gotten the lead-silver waybill from their grandfather, who had found the mine on his walk Westward. And grandpa kept a pretty accurate journal. But, it wasn't accurate enough.

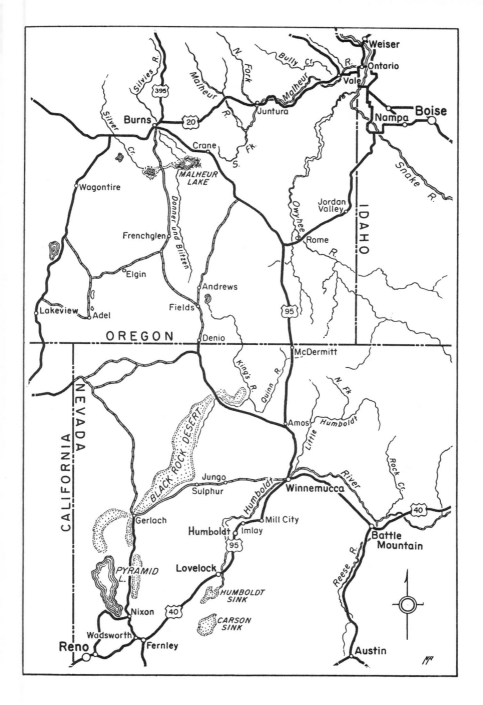

The Desert Queen

THERE IS GOLD throughout the Low Desert, from San Gorgonio Pass down the Santa Rosa Mountains, across the Salton Trough to the Chocolate Mountains and on to the Colorado River. But there is not much of it — very low grade.

W. R. Hillery (*DESERT*, December, 1953) tells the story of the Desert Queen Mine in Cathedral Canyon which leads south from Cathedral City into the San Jacinto Mountains.

The discoverer was a "young New Yorker," name unknown. The year: 1889. He worked the mine briefly, then returned East to stay. On his deathbed he gave relatives a map to the diggings which, understandably had taken on glitter as the years wore on.

In 1928, two Cathedral City men, Wilbur "Slim" Larrison and Charley Cruncleton, came across the Desert Queen — or what was later thought to be the Desert Queen.

Years pass. Then Larrison and Cruncleton heard a story from an old prospector, G. R. Hicks, that made them perk up. Hicks, it seems, had met one of the Easterner's relatives come West to make his fortune.

The clues matched. Larrison and Cruncleton excused themselves and hurried back to the mine in Cathedral Canyon. They found it without difficulty, but the ore they sampled proved rather ordinary — like all Low Desert gold. Was this the bonanza that had caused a transcontinental stir?

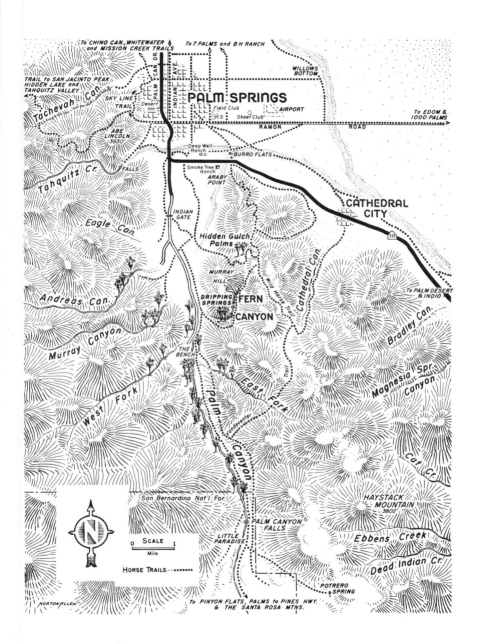

To CHINO CAN., WHITEWATER and MISSION CREEK TRAILS

To 7 PALMS and B H RANCH

WILLOWS BOTTOM

TRAIL to SAN JACINTO PEAK HIDDEN LAKE and TAHQUITZ VALLEY

Tachevah Can.

SKY LINE TRAIL

Desert Inn

PALM CAN. DR.

INDIAN AVE.

INDIAN STATE

PALM SPRINGS

Field Club
H.S.
Skeet Club
AIRPORT

To EDOM & 1000 PALMS

RAMON   ROAD

ABE LINCOLN 3830

Tahquitz Cr.   FALLS

Deep Well Ranch G.C.

BURRO FLATS

Smoke Tree Ranch

ARABY POINT

Eagle Can.

INDIAN GATE

Hidden Gulch Palms

CATHEDRAL CITY

MURRAY HILL

Andreas Can.

DRIPPING SPRINGS

FERN CANYON

Cathedral Can.

To PALM DESERT & INDIO

Bradley Can.

Murray Canyon

THE BENCH

West Fork

East Fork

Wild Horse

Palm Canyon

Magnesia Spr. Canyon

Cat Cr.

San Bernardino Nat'l. For.

HAYSTACK MOUNTAIN 3802

N

SCALE
0   1
Mile

HORSE TRAILS····

PALM CANYON FALLS

LITTLE PARADISE

Ebbens Creek

Dead Indian Cr.

POTRERO SPRING

NORTON ALLEN

To PINYON FLATS, PALMS to PINES HWY. & THE SANTA ROSA MTNS.

Wells-Fargo Gold

THERE WAS A saying in the Old West that when a Wells-Fargo stage was held-up, it was merely a case of robbers stealing from thieves—a reflection of the high freighting rates that prevailed in those distant days.

Perhaps this explains why the people of Nevada and their governor were not too harsh on an old Mexican who participated in a Wells-Fargo stick-up in the late 1800s. Three of his companions were killed in a gun fight, but the Mexican sat in prison for eight years and then was paroled. Of course, he was dying from tuberculosis, but still eight years was a short sentence in pioneer times.

The robbery took place "between the Carson River and a low swampy spot near the state prison." The stage was out of Virginia City, bound for Carson City. The year was probably 1885—sketchy prison records indicate a Mexican was arrested for robbery in the county that year.

The four *banditos* were afoot. They chased the driver and the guard down the road toward Carson, then grabbed the strong box. In it was 300 pounds of bullion: $60,000.

Four men can't carry 300 pounds of anything very far, but by the time the posse arrived—and it did not take long—the gold was buried.

The Mexican refused to *hablar*. After his release he went into Carson City to die—and did not attempt to relocate the strong box, reported the Wells-Fargo detectives assigned to trail him.

Jane Atwater's account of the Lost Wells-Fargo Gold is in *DESERT's* April, 1954, issue.

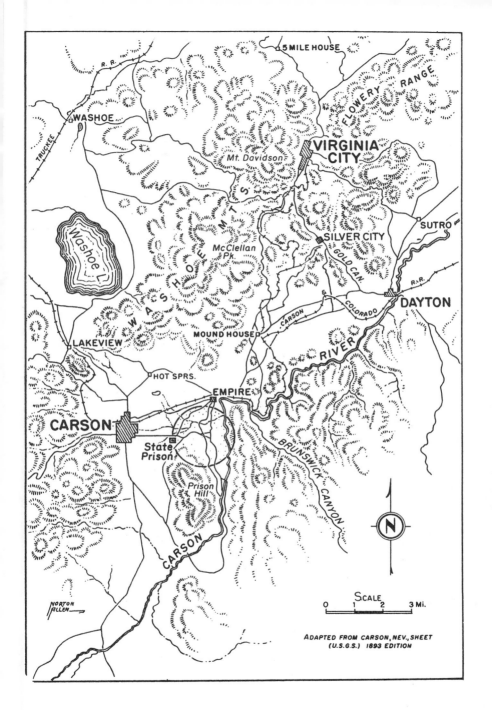

Lost Cement Mine

MARK TWAIN, J. Ross Browne and W. A. Chalfant wrote their versions of the story and in June, 1954, "Shep" Shepherd told *DESERT* readers all about it. Various sources confirm the fact that some Indians in the Owens River country had more than their share of gold. And it came, perhaps, from the fabulous Lost Cement Mine.

The cement, in this case, refers to the matrix in which the gold was found.

Shepherd's article has two travelers on the Spanish Trail being separated from a group of fellow travelers by hostile Indians. The year was 1857.

The men ran for their lives and ended up on the desert-side of the Sierra Nevadas—at the headwaters of the Owens River.

"A short time later, in the same general vicinity, they were resting near a small valley within sight of a lofty gray mountain. One man broke off a piece of cement like ledge and found it spotted with yellow flakes."

Over the mountain they went into the Central Valley where one partner promptly disappeared and the other died, but not before the latter gave his doctor, a Dr. Randall, a map to the gold.

Dr. Randall crossed the Sierras in 1861. He organized a big search team—with no luck. That is to say, *he* had no luck, but two men in his crew found the ledge. A man named Van Horn, and another—nameless, but known to be a German—quit Dr. Randall's crew on a pretext and hightailed it to Virginia City for supplies and, incidentally, a third partner.

Back they went to get down to work—but they were driven off by an Indian, Joaquin Jim. Then Van Horn became seriously ill, and retired to San Francisco. Van Horn had the feeling his partners were going to do him dirt, so he beat them to it. He blabbed, and the information came into possession of two men named Kirkpatrick and Colt. Off to the Mono country they went—where they found not gold, but the skeletons of Van Horn's late partners, victims of Joaquin Jim.

For years the Lost Cement Mine was a popular magnet. Sometimes as many as 20 parties were in the field at once.

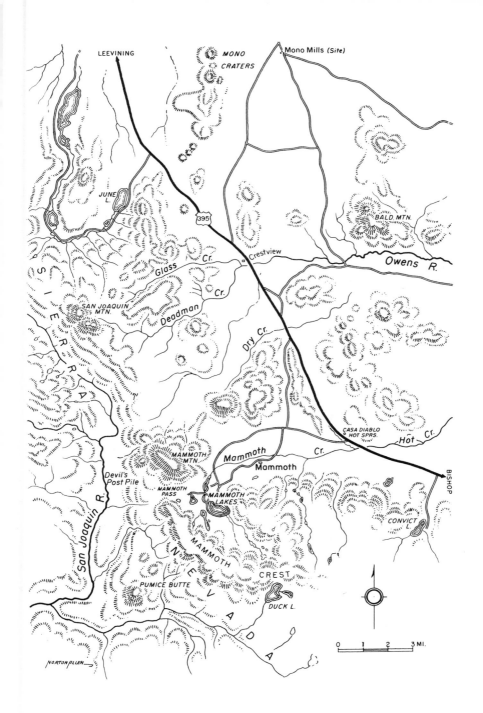

LEEVINING

MONO
CRATERS

Mono Mills (Site)

JUNE
L.

395

BALD MTN.

Crestview

Owens R.

Glass Cr.

S I E R R A

Cr.

SAN JOAQUIN
MTN.

Deadman

Dry Cr.

CASA DIABLO
HOT SPRS.

Hot Cr.

Mammoth Cr.

Mammoth

BISHOP

MAMMOTH
MTN.

Devil's
Post Pile

MAMMOTH
PASS

MAMMOTH
LAKES

San Joaquin R.

CONVICT
L.

N E V A D A

M A M M O T H
C R E S T

PUMICE BUTTE

DUCK L.

0   1   2   3 MI.

NORTON ALLEN

— 141 —

Mule Shoe Gold

SOMETIME BETWEEN 1892 and 1916 — the span of years during which the American Girl and Hedges mines were in operation — a man found and lost a fabulous gold deposit in the rugged Picacho Country on the California side of the lower Colorado River.

The man — his name is not remembered — was ill, but made a desperate attempt to reach the oasis of Dos Palmas. He was ferried across the Colorado at Picacho. Dos Palmas was 90 miles away — as the vulture flies.

Four and a half hours out of Picacho — in a saddle between two low hills (the principal source of this information once also said the hills were "high") —our friend slid off his horse and fell to the ground.

His bed, as it turned out, was a golden bonanza. ". . . he saw the golden streakings in the rock and was excited by them. He made his way to the ledge. The ore was rich beyond anything he had ever seen" — this narrative by Harold O. Weight in the September, 1954, DESERT.

The sick man took off his vest and laid it over the ledge. From the load on his pack mule, he took a mule shoe and placed it on the vest. And then the painful journey continued.

Apparently Dos Palmas was reached. The next stop was the Veteran's Hospital at Sawtelle, from which the prospector did not emerge alive.

Enter now William M. Smith. From the prospector, Smith learns the story of the Lost Mule Shoe Gold, even receives a map.

In 1927, Smith buys the property at the old Hoge Ferry, renames it the 4S Ranch. During the next 10 years, he searches for the mine. Then he gives up the ranch, but returns to the desert many times during the next decade to continue the hunt. No luck. Exit Smith.

The trouble here is that it is impossible even to guess which route the sick man took. The river road north from Picacho is now submerged under the water behind Imperial Dam. Other roads — in Parra and Gavilan washes — are all but gone. The unused Indian trails have vanished.

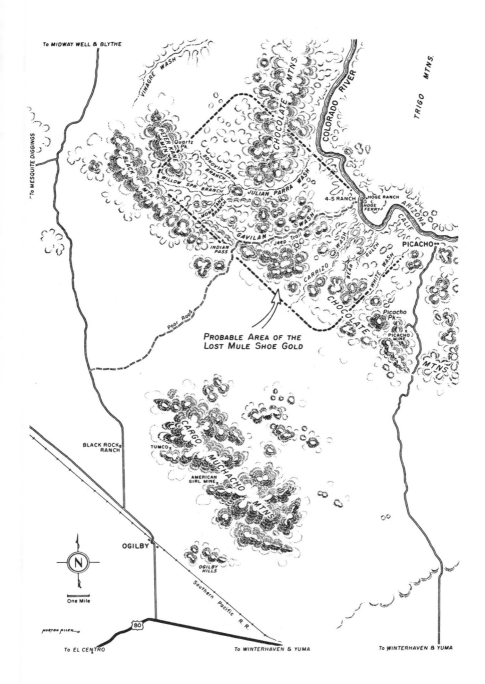

To MIDWAY WELL & BLYTHE

To MESQUITE DIGGINGS

VINAGRE WASH

PETER KANE

Quartz Pk.

BLACK MTN

SONOYA TANK BRANCH

WILLOW SPR. BRANCH

NORTH TANK BRANCH

JULIAN PARRA WASH

GAVILAN WASH

INDIAN PASS

Jeep trail

CHOCOLATE MTNS.

COLORADO RIVER

TRIGO MTNS.

4-S RANCH

HOGE RANCH & HOGE FERRY

ARIZONA

CALIF

PICACHO

CARRIZO WASH

BEAR GULCH

WHITE WASH

CHOCOLATE

Picacho Pk.

PICACHO MINE

MTNS

Poor Road

↑
PROBABLE AREA OF THE
LOST MULE SHOE GOLD

BLACK ROCK RANCH

CARGO

TUMCO

MUCHACHO

AMERICAN GIRL MINE

MTNS

Southern Pacific R.R.

OGILBY

OGILBY HILLS

N

One Mile

NORTON ALLEN

80

To EL CENTRO

To WINTERHAVEN & YUMA

To WINTERHAVEN & YUMA

Black Mesa Placer

THIS STORY Is simplicity itself. In the spring of 1916, two old Mexican brothers arrived in the Black Canyon area north of Phoenix with map in hand. Their *papa* had taken a rich load of placer gold out of this country; later he drew a map for his sons.

The map "showed a high mesa flanked by rugged hills and a winding stream to the east of it. It lay at the edge of a large rolling plain, another stream running along its eastern edge, No cities or towns were shown."

In fact, much of the information the brothers carried had been given to them orally by their *mamacita.* She told them that the placer was "about 50 miles north of a place she believed to be Phoenix, and to the west of a creek that paralleled the road." (She refers to the old road, still traceable in places.)

The Mexicans looked, found nothing. A local rancher heard their tale, studied the map, and remembered an old placer operation he had seen in the canyon. He could not retrace his steps.

There has been much gold taken from this canyon, but the big pocket undoubtedly remains.

The story in the October, 1954, *DESERT,* is by E. C. Thoroman.

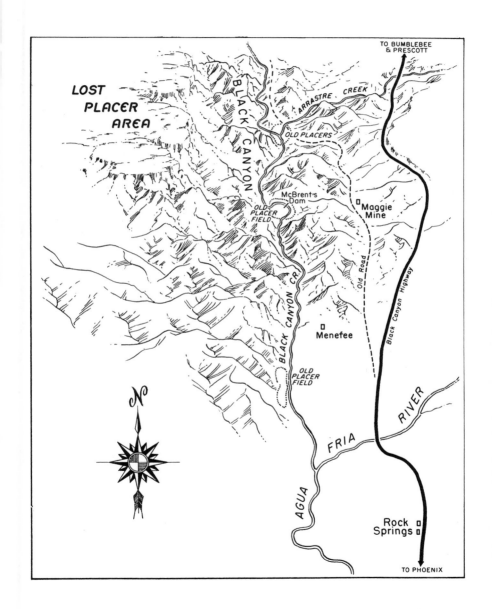

Gold of Oriflamme

THE SUMMER OF 1914 had been a scorcher, and in September rancher Chatty Helm of Valley Center, California, decided to move his milk cows to Imperial Valley where the feed situation was better.

He hired two riders, a mission Indian, Julian Cabrias, and a gangling youth, Harry Yarnell. The Indian enlivened the lonely evening campfires with stories about the country through which they were slowly passing. His stories emphasized the desert's mineral treasures.

Cabrias found an all-ears audience in Yarnell, who had more than a touch of gold fever in his bones. The young cowboy spent much of his time between jobs prospecting the backcountry.

The three men moved the cattle down San Felipe Valley, following the old Butterfield Stage road. By the third night the herd was in Earthquake Valley.

Cabrias was sent out to quiet the cows, and when he returned to camp he took Yarnell aside and showed him a handful of nuggets. The largest was the size of a peanut.

"Yarnell and the Indian walked together in the growing gloom to a place half an hour from camp (they were camped in the shadow of the hump backed Oriflamme Mountains). Cabrias stopped at the mouth of a small draw. In the rainy season a stream probably rushed down out of this small canyon, but now it was dry and barren."

It was "a short walk" from this point upcanyon to where the nuggets lay scattered on the sand. But it was too dark to go gold hunting, so Yarnell contented himself with building a small rock cairn at the mouth of the canyon on his way back out.

The cow drive resumed in the morning, and Cabrias, whose prestige has risen sharply with his nugget display of the night before, bragged to his young companion that "another place of much gold" existed to the west, over beyond Pine Valley.

In El Centro, Yarnell was offered a job which he could not refuse, and so he did not immediately return to the Oriflammes. Even worse, he talked

to a prospector in Riverside, said prospector immediately disappearing out of town, desert-bound.

Young Yarnell, back in Earthquake Valley the following spring, could not find cairn nor right canyon.

What is more, in Banner he was greeted with the news that a prospector, George Benton by name, had found a $3000 chunk of gold in Pine Valley — the "other place of much gold."

Russ Leadabrand was author of *DESERT's* November, 1954, article.

Jabonero Waybill

AN ARIZONA MAN named Benjamin Byrd gave Harold O. Weight a remarkable document — the directions to a lost gold ledge in the Camino del Diablo country along the Arizona-Sonora border.

Many men have searched for the gold — some have lost their lives in the quest.

El Jabonero — the soapmaker — became partners with two fellow Mexicans who were returning from the big excitement of the California Gold Rush.

Here is the version of the story Jose Alvarado of Yuma told Weight (*DESERT*, January, 1955). (Alvarado had twice searched for the mine in company with an old man whose father had known El Jabonero.)

The two Mexican miners went from Tinajas Altas to the Tule Tank. From this point they took the old trail to Sonoyta. "They followed it until late at night and made a dry camp."

That night the horses wandered from camp, and one of them had broken his hobble and disappeared. Next morning one of the Mexicans, trailing the animal, came to a hillside scattered with gold nuggets.

The men were reunited at Agua Salada where they revealed the happy situation that they felt certain would make them wealthy beyond belief. They needed supplies and pack animals — which they obtained from El Jabonero in Sonoyta. In exchange the soapmaker was given a full partnership.

The trio backtracked as far as Agua Salada where they were waylaid by wild Papagos. The two miners were killed; El Jabonero severely wounded. In fact, his injuries led to blindness.

There is another version of this story, contained in a letter supposedly written by one C. O. Bustamente. The essential difference is that a gold ledge was located on the central peak of a group of three — "called the *Tinajera* by the prospector — which stood alone on open ground." According to Senor Bustamente, the Indian attack occurred at the foot of these peaks. As a youth, Bustamente knew El Jabonero in Los Angeles. The old blind soapmaker dictated a waybill to the gold on September 27, 1878. Bus-

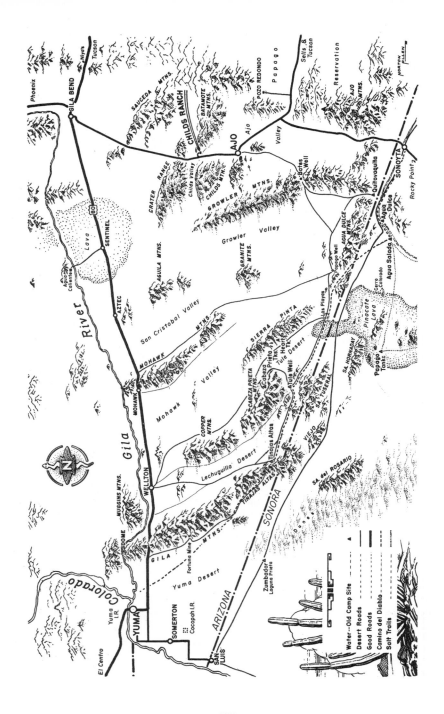

— 150 —

tamente's father fell heir to the waybill, and a copy of this document was given to writer Weight by Benjamin Byrd.

Here is the waybill in Weight's possession:

First Call: Leave Quitobaquito following the old road leading to *Tinajas Altas* (High Tanks).

Second Call: Thence to the end (*punta*) of Pinto Mountains.

Third Call: From Pinto Mountains go to Cabeza Prieta Mountain.

Fourth Call: At Cabeza Prieta there is a well of water.

Fifth Call: After leaving Quitobaquito following this imaginary line pass or cross an arroyo at a place where the road forks out for the first time, one leading to Tinajas Altas and the other to Mohawk or the Gila River.

Sixth Call: By standing at the forks of the road to the right three peaks standing alone are seen and in direction to said peaks the middle one is the mine on the opposite side of it.

Seventh Call: From the said forks in the direction said peaks down in the arroyo there is a big flat rock in the form of a table with crow bars pointing to the peaks of the said mine.

Eighth Call: We were killed at the foot of said peaks of said mine. The little peaks cannot be seen from no other place but only from the fork of the old road leading from Quitobaquito to Tinajas Altas. On the other side of the middle peak there is water and there is where the gold is.

Ninth Call: You must have great care in locating the fork of the roads because that is the only point from where the peaks can be seen and cannot be seen from no other place.

Tenth Call: In order for you to make sure, find from the old folks at Sonoita which is the old road leading from Quitobaquito to Tinajas Altas. It must be blotted out after so many years.

Eleventh Call: And all I ask is that if you find the mine you help my daughter. This is my last will and testament, wherefore I witnesseth with my signature.

El Jabonero

Hardin Silver

THIS IS EITHER the greatest sleeper in Western mining — or a swindle that ranks with the Great Diamond Hoax (see page 186). Author Nell Murbarger (April, 1955, *DESERT*) is of the opinion that it is the latter — the Lost Hardin Silver is a phony — and yet . . .

A '49er, J. A. Hardin, was one of a party of three hunters who made the original discovery. They stumbled upon "a deposit of soft material, similar to volcanic ash . . . (with) glittering bits of stone scattered on the surface."

California glittered a lot more than did pretty rocks in the middle of a truly forbidding desert, so when the hunters rejoined their wagon train at Mud Meadows, the decision was to continue westward without delay.

Hardin settled in Petaluma, but returned to the Black Rock country in 1858. He used Double Hot Springs as a base camp, but had no luck finding his silver bonanza.

And then a prospector who had seen the "black, waxy-looking ore" from Idaho's rich Poorman Mine discovered somewhat similar ore in the Black Rock, and the rush was on. Hardin's Silver had been found, or so the mining world believed.

One problem remained: how to extract the silver from the ore. All attempts failed. Then someone remembered that "similar ore" was being worked in Freiberg, Germany, as well as at the Poorman, so a sample was sent to Charles Isenbeck, a leading Freiberg chemist. Unfortunately, Isenbeck was probably a leading Freiberg crook, too.

His report said the Black Rock ore was rich — perhaps 25 percent silver. Given time and money — two years at $1000 a month — Isenbeck felt sure he could work out a simple method of separating the silver from its matrix.

Northern Nevada opinion was divided. Half the population wanted to build a solid silver monument to Isenbeck. The other half wanted to build a gallows.

The two years stretched to seven and then Isenbeck announced he

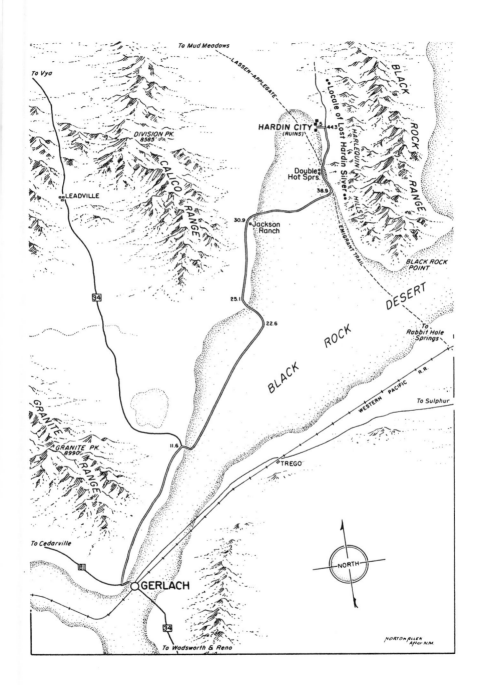

To Mud Meadows

To Vya

LASSEN-APPLEGATE

BLACK

DIVISION PK.
8585'

HARDIN CITY
(RUINS)

Locale of Lost Hardin Silver

443'

ROCK

HARLEQUIN HILLS

CALICO RANGE

RANGE

LEADVILLE

Double
Hot Sprs.

38.9

Jackson
Ranch

30.9

EMIGRANT TRAIL

BLACK ROCK
POINT

34

25.1

DESERT

22.6

ROCK

To
Rabbit Hole
Springs

BLACK

GRANITE

WESTERN   PACIFIC   R.R.

To Sulphur

GRANITE PK.
8990'

11.6

RANGE

TREGO

To Cedarville

NORTH

81

GERLACH

34

To Wadsworth & Reno

NORTON ALLEN
After N.M.

— 153 —

was ready to go into large-scale production of his "secret flux" and would like the Black Rock miners to ship him 13 tons of ore, which they did.

The letter from Germany set hopes soaring once again. Isenbeck had extracted values up to $400 per ton. A mill was built (to be managed by the chemist) and two others were started, and Hardin City began growing up around them. It was a poor time for Isenbeck to disappear, but disappear he did — and so did Hardin City.

Were the rocks Hardin found and the "black waxy-looking ore" one and the same? It's a big, big country.

Hidden Gold of Bicuner

HAROLD O. WEIGHT builds a strong case for the Hidden Gold of Bicuner in the June, 1955, *DESERT*.

The facts would give considerable credence to the possibility of this Spanish mission treasure having existed, but, as Weight says in the article, this is a "most hopelessly lost treasure."

Franciscan padres in 1870 established two mission-pueblos in the Lower Colorado region — one on Fort Yuma Hill; the other upriver, near the site of present-day Laguna Dam. The latter was Mission San Pedro y San Pablo de Bicuner, henceforth referred to as Bicuner.

The Spaniards laid out their church-centered town in what later became the fabulously rich Potholes Gold Placers area. And across the river, awaiting the hungry gold-seekers of another age, lay the equally rich Laguna Gold Placers.

It would seem, if we believe all the stories we hear, that every mission in the New World was founded on or near a secret gold mine. In the case of Bicuner, there can be little doubt that this was the case — except that there was nothing secret about this gold. It crops up in many historic accounts, and later was extensively mined.

During Bicuner's eight months of life, the biggest surface nuggets were undoubtedly gathered-up and brought to the mission where, for the first time, the Quechan Indians could trade these pretty rocks for something useful. According to one source, the big business was in beans — one plate of beans for one gold nugget.

On July 17, 1781, the Quechans had had enough of the Spaniards and their beans, and put the mission to the torch. Padre Francisco Garces was martyred in this uprising.

What of Bicuner's treasury? Some say the missionaries, sensing trouble, put the gold in cowhides and buried it. Others say the Indians tossed it into the Colorado River.

Hundreds of people have looked and dug for Bicuner's gold in and near the mission site. But Jose Alvarado of Yuma gave author Weight a new

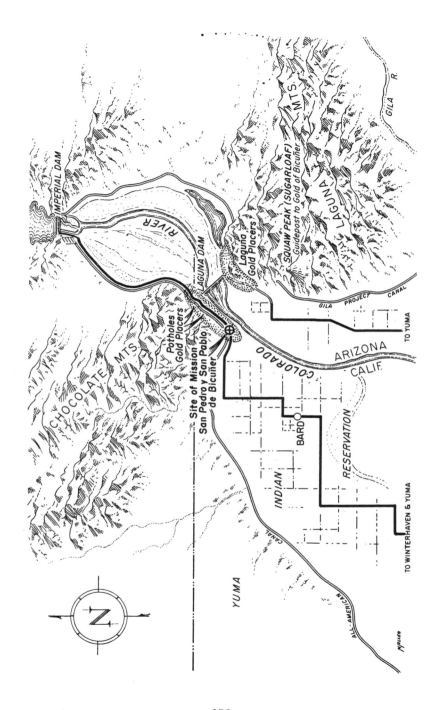

angle. According to Alvarado, he was told that the gold was taken "across the river and down to the big peak."

When the Indians assembled on the "flat in front of the picacho" the gold was buried in a big hole.

The Arizona peak in question is named Sugarloaf on the U.S.G.S. Laguna quadrangle. Locally, it is known as Squaw Peak. From Arizona Highway 95 it resembles a perfect cone.

Dark Gold on the Tabaseca

THIS STORY BEGINS around the turn of the century at the rich Mesquite Diggings gold fields east of Glamis. It is told by Harold O. Weight in the July, 1955, *DESERT*.

A terminal case tubercular known only as "Slim" wandered into the camp one day. At that time, miner Tom Clark was taking out as much as $90 a day from his claim at Mesquite. Generous Tom gave the unfortunate Slim two $20 gold pieces and some advice: It was a big desert, and there was a great deal of gold yet to be discovered. "Maybe farther up along the Chocolates . . . go out and see what you can find."

Slim hired a burro pack outfit and started off to make his fortune. Weight outlines his itinerary: "From Glamis . . . he trailed northwest along the . . . Chocolate Mountains. He halted for a while at Heyden — or Heyburn — Well. He rounded the point and entered . . . Salvation Pass, camping at Salvation Spring. (His route here is now part of the aerial gunnery range.) From Salvation Spring he trekked northeastward, passing entirely through the Chocolates. Some time thereafter he . . . camped at Chuckawalla Well at the base of the Little Chuckawallas."

The burros liked it here, but Slim had to push on. He gathered-up the animals and "followed either the old Indian trail or the almost abandoned Bradshaw stage and freight route, traveling westerly to Tabaseca Tank . . ."

The burros bolted and returned to Chuckawalla Well. Slim followed, went through a second round-up, and once again headed for the water at Tabaseca. Only this time his strength was nearly gone. From Tabeseca he set his sights for Dos Palmas near the railroad. Weight says he traveled an Indian trail.

"Somewhere along the trail, where it crossed an elevation, he sat down to rest. He noticed the earth around him was very red . . . Slim filled a sack with it, loaded the sack on a burro, and continued along the trail."

Later at Dos Palmas he discovered the sack of ore had $120 worth of gold in it. But Slim was dying and all the gold in the desert could not buy him a year or a month or even a week of life.

Remembering his last benefactor, Tom Clark, Slim put a third of

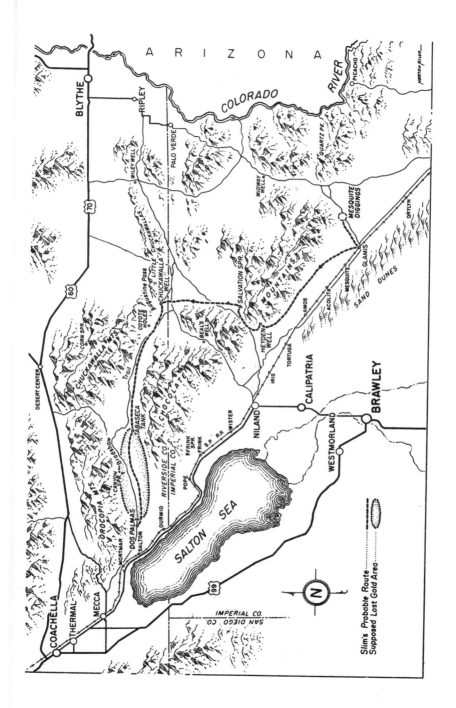

the gold and a crude map in an envelope and mailed it off to Mesquite Diggings. He died before Tom arrived.

Tom had rushed to Dos Palmas to comfort the friendless man, not to milk him of his knowledge of the new placer field. Tom's Mesquite Diggings placer was still producing more than enough gold, and so Tom returned to the bird-in-hand, forsaking the two-in-the-bush.

Years later, Tom's home in the Palo Verde Valley was robbed and searched three successive times. Had someone in Dos Palmas gotten wind of Slim's gold?

In 1942, Tom took the bus from Blythe to visit friends and relatives in Los Angeles. Somewhere on that trip he vanished — and with him went the knowledge of where Slim's crude map was cached. Tom was then 84 years of age.

Some people who know the story of the rough, blackened gold nuggets, suggest that instead of starting from Tabaseca Tanks on his discovery trip, Slim actually was at the Coyote Holes.

The October, 1955, *DESERT* carried a letter from John J. Adams of Crestline, Calif.: "I can confirm some of the details of Harold Weight's story . . . I was contracting desert assessment work near Dos Palmas in 1909 and knew the party called Slim. I received several of the nuggets mentioned in the story in payment for work I did on a stationary engine at a mine a few miles to the north . . ."

––––––––––––––

IN THE AUGUST, 1939, *DESERT*, Randall Henderson describes a small gold mining operation in the southern spur of the Chocolates north of Glamis. The Van Derpoels, father and son, were working "$5000 ore" at the Mary Lode Mine. There are plenty of placer fields in the Chocolates (eastern end), but to Henderson's knowledge, this was the first lode claim in the mountains "worth the shoe leather it took to find it."

––––––––––––––

IN 1914, A MAN named Ebner and a companion were driving packed burros across the desert from Picacho westward.

"Somewhere before they dropped down into Mammoth Wash leading to the Salton Sea, they came to a place . . . littered with pieces of heavy metal." This quote from Seward White (*DESERT*, November, 1953).

The metal was native copper, and author White joined Ebner on a search for it in 1933. They blistered their feet — and got nothing more for their efforts. Base camp for the search was Pegleg Well which White describes as an old copper shaft.

The Russell-Huhn Ledge

ASA M. RUSSELL'S story was published in the September, 1955, *DESERT*. It is my opinion (supported by the fact that no article published before or since in the magazine — on any subject — has drawn as much favorable mail) that this is the finest lost mine story ever to appear in *DESERT*. First of all, it is an honest first-person account of a logical mining operation. Secondly, the reader is given insight into the techniques of prospecting. Thirdly, it is a story about a real human being with whom the reader can join in celebration and sorrow. And lastly, it is well written.

Mr. Russell — known in the Death Valley country as "Panamint Russ" — has kindly given his consent to the unabridged reprinting of his *DESERT* article:

ERNIE HUHN, or Siberian Red as he was known by his friends, is gone now. He passed away a few years ago and is buried at Shoshone, east of Death Valley. He was fairly well off financially when he died because of the interest he had in the well run Grantham Talc Mine.

But Ernie could have been one of the richest men on earth and me along with him if — and that's a mighty small if!

While he lived I dared not tell of our experience high in the Panamint Range in 1925, but now I'm sure he wouldn't mind if I do. He was very touchy about it saying that if anyone ever found out they would class us as fools. I guess he was right, but he should have made it "careless fools."

Folks wondered why Ernie, who had mined gold in Siberia, Alaska and California and loved the yellow metal as much as any man, suddenly gave up looking for it and satisfied himself instead by opening up drifts of plain baby talcum powder, as he called it. I was his partner and the last man to grubstake him on a gold venture. I know why.

I met Siberian Red at the Cresta Escavada (summit diggings), a placer property near Randsburg in the early 1920s. The terrain there was made up of rolling, spotted bedrock with no paydirt, just egg shaped rocks. Although it mined out to a dollar a yard Ernie soon found that it wouldn't float a dredge so he decided to move on. There was no way to make it pay.

We met again in Trona some time later and during our visit he repeatedly gazed intently at the towering Panamint Range visible behind the Slate

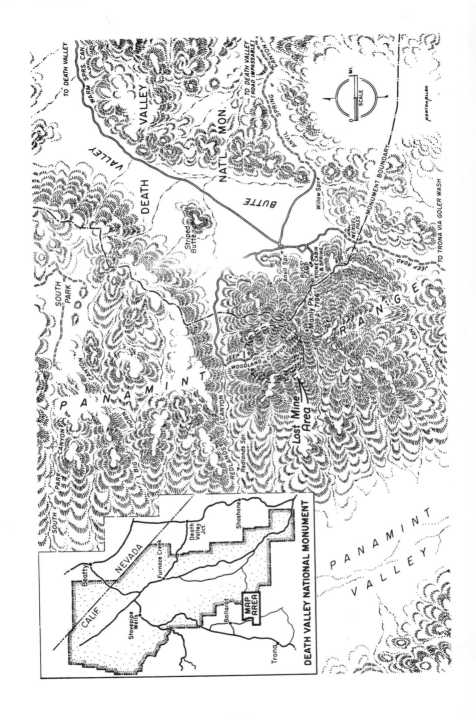

Range. Finally he remarked, "I understand that four formations meet there at the south end of the Panamints. It should be a hot spot to prospect." Somewhere Ernie found out that a road could be easily cut from Death Valley up to Anvil Canyon opening that area for mining if and when a discovery was made. At Anvil Springs there was a stone house and plenty of water.

"Carl Mengel, who has only one leg, says he came through there with his burros — stayed at the stone house and says the area looks like good gold country to him," Ernie went on. I soon became enthusiastic about the area's prospects and offered to grubstake him on the trip and to accompany him, too. I had a fairly successful tree business in Los Angeles at that time and could afford the venture. Before long we struck an agreement.

I bought a truck, loaded it with supplies enough for three months and we headed for Butte Valley by way of Death Valley. In those days there was an old road through Death Valley with a sign post pointed toward the mountains which read: "Butte Valley, 21 Miles." Instead of going on to Butte, the road ended right there in a soft sandy wash where the water drained down to Death Valley through the narrow canyon.

We returned to our original plan and headed up Anvil Canyon making our own road. Every thousand feet we had to stop and drag off the rocks to clear the next thousand feet ahead. To get through the loose gravel we used block and tackle. After five days of hard work we had our road into Butte Canyon by way of Anvil Canyon. The former takes its name from a strata of solid rock projecting 500 feet high in the center of this valley. There was no dirt or vegetation on this huge rock and it was striped with many different colors. The miners called it the Striped Butte.

We located the spring and the stone house and set up camp. We were never able to find out who built the house, but it was built to last. It dated back to the early 1880s and was as good as ever. Here we relaxed for a couple of days, taking short walks around camp.

We had a beautiful view down the canyon to the floor of Death Valley, 20 miles below. The refreshing breeze picked up the scent of sage, ephreda and pinyon making our campsite a delightful place.

The country immediately around us was well mineralized. Small veins shot out across the hills in all directions. Some looked like they would pan fairly good and had they been wider would have caused plenty of excitement. The stone house contained some old newspapers and books, pack saddles and odd shaped demijohns, reminders of days that had gone before. We had ideal prospecting headquarters.

We soon found that this was a big area to cover. Naturally we concentrated on the valley floor at first, prospecting a day and then resting a day.

We wanted to toughen up gradually before we tackled the high ground. On these low level hikes Ernie would often reach down to the ground with his pick and crack open a rock that looked like ordinary mud to me. He explained that after a little experience I too could distinguish mere mud from stones that had been thinly covered with mud following a rain.

Occasionally I picked up a piece of float. Each time I did Ernie knocked it from my hand and warned me that it was a bad habit to get into. "Unless you intend to follow the float up and find out where it comes from, don't waste your time and mine. You might have a piece that dropped out of a saddle bag or a pack mule. Be sure your sample comes off a vein of ore in place — and a vein wide enough to investigate. Remember, we are 67 miles from the nearest supplies. Don't waste time." I listened to his advice. I knew it was experience talking and I had much to learn.

In time we became tanned and toughened. Our legs were strong. Ernie was convinced that somewhere along this contact a rich vein existed.

One day we had a visitor — a Shoshone Indian — who was leading a string of pack burros. He was on his way to Warm Springs to do a little prospecting. He told us that if we needed some packing in the near future, he would be glad to do it for us.

Another week went by and on the first of October a tall, unshaven man named Greenslit walked into our camp. He was a tough old fellow of 65 and had been prospecting the hills for six days out of Trona.

He took out a piece of ore and showed it to us. He had found it on the ridge near Manly peak in a short tunnel of an abandoned mine. He relocated it and was on his way now to Shoshone to try to interest some friends in his find.

After he had gone the next morning Ernie took the piece of ore Greenslit had given him and panned it out. He found it to run about $200 to the ton.

"I wonder just exactly where he got that rock?" I asked. By the look on Ernie's face I knew he was wondering the same thing. He pointed to the high ridge to the right of Manly Peak. "It must be up there," he said. He scanned the area with his field glasses and then handed them to me. "Look close up there — there's a little gray patch on the mountain side —

looks like an old dump — that may be where Greenslit found his ore."

The next day we tried the higher ground. Ernie warned me before we left that when we reached the timber line our vision would be cut down considerably except in small and infrequent clearings. He had me prepare 10 pieces of five different colored rags and told me that should I find a vein large enough to locate, I was to mark it properly, take one piece of colored cloth and wrap the sample in it and number it. The matching piece of rag I was to tie on the top of the highest and nearest tree. A small strip of the cloth was to be tied at ground level. If, after panning the ore, we found it to be worth while, the vein would be easy to relocate. I was also instructed to make a note of the general terrain around my find. "This is the best system I know of for tenderfoot prospectors," Ernie said to me as we started out at dawn.

It was a steep climb up the hogback to Manly Peak, but we took our time and had no trouble reaching the saddle on the ridge at the right of the peak before noon. The view alone was worth the climb. Looking over the Slate Range toward Trona the Panamint Valley lay at our feet and at our backs was Death Valley.

We ate lunch on the ridge and then made our way to the gray patch below the saddle. As Ernie had predicted we found that it was an old ore dump and there, nearby, was Greenslit's new monument. An old anvil and a few scattered tools with rotted wooden handles lay near the tunnel mouth. We guessed that its former owner was an old timer who had found the high altitude detrimental to his mining efforts.

Before we separated, Ernie gave me my instructions for the prospecting trip back to camp. He was going to cover the lower side, close to the contact, while I was to stay up along the side hill. If I needed him I was to yell as loud as I could — the air was clear and my voice would carry. If I found anything sensational I was to let him know at once.

We started off and for a time I could hear him cracking rocks with his pick. I made my way around some large boulders, keeping my eye out for snakes, outcroppings and quartz veins and all the time trying to remember all I had been taught during the past weeks by Ernie.

The little veins made me mad as they peeked out under ledges. I followed them down draws, out under ledges and up steep slopes. Few were wide enough to get excited about. Still I took some samples from the widest ones and marked them as ordered.

About four in the afternoon I ran across an outcropping of yellow broken quartz under a pinyon tree. The vein, the widest I had ever seen, was about 15 inches across. It was heavy with iron oxide and I figured important enough to call Ernie.

I yelled down the canyon and presently he answered. It took him 30 minutes to find me. After studying the vein he gave me his verdict: "pretty high up, rugged approach, should run about $40 a ton. It would have to widen out considerably to be profitable."

I was disappointed, but he suggested I put up a monument, locate, and mark it well for perhaps someday the price of gold would go up and then it would be worth mining this vein.

I showed him the rest of my samples, all wrapped carefully in their colored cloths and numbered. He didn't comment on them, but told me that we would pan them out on Sunday. He reached into his pockets and pulled out a half dozen pieces of rock. One of them was cement gray in color and was very heavy. I showed surprise at the weight and asked him about it.

He had chipped it off a vein about three feet wide. The ledge was only exposed for about 20 feet on the surface on the steep side of the draw near the contact. Although he had never heard of anyone finding platinum in these mountains, he wondered if the sample he had might not contain some of that precious metal.

I asked him if I could use his glass to give the specimen a close look, but he had forgotten it. "We'll pan it Sunday along with the other stuff," he said and started off toward camp.

"Did you mark it with a colored cloth?" I shouted after him.

Ernie laughed. "That's only for rookies. An old timer remembers and doesn't need flags and sign posts."

When we got back to our stone house the moon was up. After a sound sleep we decided we had better rest for two days before tackling any high ground again. I placed all the samples we brought back on the high shelf on the outside of the house and we agreed to pan them out as soon as possible. It's a good pastime when you are laying around camp. But we were out of fresh meat and spent a day hunting and then on the next day there were shoes to sole, wood to cut and other chores around camp. On the third day we tended the small garden we had put in earlier near the spring, so we put off panning the specimens again.

Then we had visitors. A couple of miners took the road we had made to camp. They were out looking over the country and we spent many hours talking to them around the campfire. When Sunday came again we spent it quail hunting and that night the four of us enjoyed a delicious dinner.

Our supplies were running low so after the miners left Ernie and I took a week off and went into Shoshone to stock up again. We didn't hurry and still another week went by before we picked up the specimens to pan them out. By now over three weeks had slipped by.

Ernie breezed through my six colored cloth wrapped samples and a few of his own before noon. We found nothing to excite us. The whole lot averaged about $25 a ton. The rock from the vein I had called him to see under the pinyon tree was the best — it ran around $40.

After lunch I ground up the heavy cement gray stone and Ernie started to pan it out. He remarked that he wouldn't be surprised to find a little platinum in it.

I had ground it up well as Ernie had asked me to do. Coarse pieces of iron may often hold small particles of gold that had to be released if a good pan was to be had.

While Ernie panned the gray stone I sat on a large rock near camp and took some pot shots at a hawk that was circling low trying to scare a family of quail out in the open.

An explosive yell from Ernie brought my thoughts back into focus and I slid off the boulder and ran toward him. He was jumping up and down with glee and shouting, "We hit it! We hit! We hit it!"

"Look at the gold," he cried holding out the pan to me. I grabbed it from him and still dazed peered into it. The bottom was covered with gold.

Ernie was excited and spoke on in a frenzied voice: "I knew it — I knew I would find something good on the contact! We hit it this time, Russ! Our troubles are over! We're rich! We're rich! I never saw ore like that any place in the world!"

After he calmed down he told me that the panning indicated an ore value of $15,000 a ton! "And just think, it's ready money — free milling. The ground it all open for location. How does it feel to be rich, Russ? How does it feel to be able to have anything you want — and plenty of good yellow gold to pay for it?"

I couldn't answer — it had all been so sudden. I walked into the house and in a fog put on the spuds and beans for supper.

That meal was the longest I have ever eaten. It started at 5:30 in the afternoon and at 2 the next morning we were still at the table dreaming and talking. Ernie had a list a mile long of things he was going to buy with his new found wealth. At the very top was a Lincoln coupe, half way down was a small yacht — he was going to sail to the old country and see his mother — bring her back to this country with him. He was walking on air.

Clearing off the table at 2:30 in the morning I could hardly believe it had hapened to me. Then I felt a little sick in my stomach remembering that we had let three weeks slip by following discovery, and in those three weeks there had been a heavy rain and a few light showers.

Ernie first spotted the 20 feet of gray ledge from which the specimen came while resting on a boulder somewhere on that vast mountain. The mountain side was steep and the ledge would be hard to find. How much better would I have felt that night had Ernie used colored cloth to mark the gray stone's vein.

Neither Ernie nor I could sleep. He paced the floor eager for daybreak to arrive. He was all packed, ready to go. He had powder, fuse, steel tape, blanket, location papers — everything he would need. While he was hunting for the ledge I was going to go into Warm Springs to buy a pair of pack burros. We would need them to carry supplies for a new camp near our new mine.

Ernie would put up the discovery monument and locate it and pack back what ore he could. When I showed up with the burros we would return to the mine and put up the corner markers.

As soon as it was light enough to see he was put out the door. "Get those burros up here quick as you can," he shouted over his shoulder as he started up the hill.

Twenty hours later — near midnight — he returned to the stone house. Something had gone wrong. His clothes were torn and his face haggard. He slumped into a chair by the fireplace and muttered four words: "I couldn't find it."

There was nothing for me to say. I turned to the stove and started to warm up some food for him. As I did my eyes fell upon the colored cloth on the shelf I had used to mark my worthless veins.

He was gone before I woke up the next morning. That night he staggered in again. Nothing. This went on for days and weeks.

I went along with him several times, but my prospecting partner was not the same man. He rushed from bush to boulder — nervous, excited, cursing and damning the elements that had taunted him with a peek at a treasure and then concealed it again.

I took him to all the places I had marked with the colored rags which were easy to find, thinking that he might, in some way, get above the spot he was looking for, recognize a familiar rock or tree and somehow find that gray ledge again. But, it was no use. His nerves were cracking. He had to quit.

For about three months he remained at Butte Valley and looked for the ledge and then he left it for good. Ernie landed at Warm Springs and got back into talc mining.

We often met in Shoshone in later years and he would always bring up the subject of the lost mine. "Is there anything we overlooked? Have you searched for the ledge since then?" he would invariably ask me.

My guess is that the rains that fell after he picked up the specimen caused a boulder to roll off the top of the mountain across the ledge, pushing the soft decomposed granite ahead of it over the vein. The rain and the wind could have left that small area completely changed in three weeks.

I went back to the city to work at my old job, but every year since have returned to the mountains to do assessment work on my claims. I often wonder how long it will be before someone stumbles across that rich vein on the southwest slope of Manly Peak facing Redland Canyon. If it is hidden, I wonder if nature will expose it again for some prospector — more alert than we were — to claim. The ground is still open for location.

Folks ask me, "how can you lose a mine?" How do you lose anything? Through carelessness.

Algodones Gold

THE ALGODONES DUNES are from two to six-plus miles wide and more than 40 miles in length. Some of the individual sand mountains are 300 feet above mesa level. It is an imposing barrier — a bit of the Sahara Desert in California.

In June, 1917, an unnamed prospector left Mexicali headed for the gold country at the Cargo Muchacho Mountains. At Gray's Well, on the western edge of the Algodones, he shunned the old plank road and turned due north into the sandy wilderness.

A mile north of Gray's, the prospector turned east through a low pass in the dunes. (Another information source says he turned east at the second pass north of "Highway Pass" through which the plank road ran.)

The lone traveler was caught in a sandstorm that stripped him of his burro, water, and all supplies.

After the wind died, he staggered across a bed of caliche — hardpan. The flat, hard depressions are common in dune country, created where pockets of rainwater collect and cement the sands and clays.

But, this was no ordinary stretch of hardpan. Scattered over its surface were gold nuggets. The prospector collected 17 pounds of gold and then continued his desperate hike.

At Ogilby on the railroad, he was cared for by the telegraph operator and then put on the Los Angeles train.

The summer ordeal in the dunes cost the prospector his life, but before he died, he drew a map to the golden drylake for a friend, said friend showing up late in 1917 at G. A. Rodenbaugh's general store in Winterhaven.

The friend made three tries for the gold, the last taking place in 1919. On each of his sallies he hired a Yuma welldigger, O. T. Willis, and his truck.

Chief information source for Harold O. Weight's article in the October, 1955, *DESERT*, was storekeeper Rodenbaugh (later to become postmaster of Winterhaven).

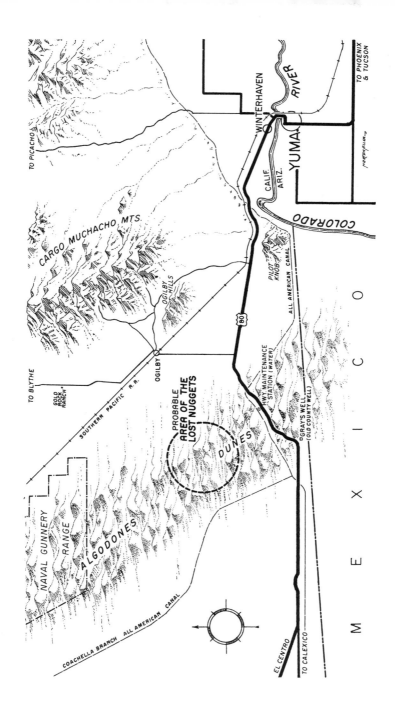

Jarbidge Sheepherder

THIS IS THE STORY of the Lost Sheepherder Mine, as much a part of Nevada as gambling and divorce. But there are many versions of this legend, some radically different from others. The variation told by Nell Murbarger in the November, 1955, *DESERT,* is traced directly to the statement made by Mrs. John Pence in 1910. Because Mrs. Pence was the wife of the man to whom the sheepherder told his story, many believe this version to be the most authentic.

The first gold to come out of this broken up-and-down country in the Jarbidge region was reported in the late 1870s. Later in 1908, a big strike created Jarbidge, now only a shadow of its former self.

In 1890, a prospector known as Ross followed some float which was very promising. In fact, we are told the ore was "fantastically rich."

The dark clouds heralding winter drove him out of the high mountains, and on his way he stopped at one of John Pence's sheep camps, where a sheepherder named Ishman was in charge.

Ross was loose-tongued. He told Ishman about the float, described where he had left pick and shovel to mark the highest point to which he had tracked the surface gold.

The following spring when Ishman returned to the high country, he steered his herd to Ross' claim. The pick and shovel and the gold were there — and so was a whitening human skeleton.

Ishman spent the summer tracing the float higher into the mountain, and in time found a "small cropping of rock thickly seamed with yellow."

The sheepherder returned to Pence's ranch with a couple of mementos of his summer's outing: a few pieces of gold ore and the skeleton's skull.

An assay placed the gold's value at a minimum $4000 per ton. The skull offered no clues for identification.

Next spring, the Ishman-Pence partnership made an assault on the gold ledge. Unfortunately, the sheepherder suffered a fatal stroke while hurrying up the steep mountainside. Thus fell silent the only man who had put a pick into the gold ledge.

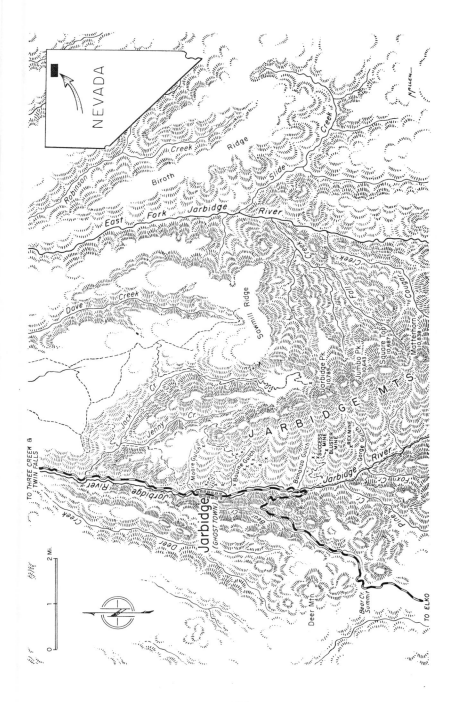

Coso Treasure Canyon

YOU'LL HAVE TO WAIT until world peace is declared before you go looking for this lost treasure. It lies within the boundaries of the Naval Ordnance Test Station at China Lake.

In the late 1920s, according to Russ Leadabrand (February, 1956, *DESERT*), prospector Frank Bishop was in the Coso-Argus country below Death Valley. One night at his cabin in Brown, an Indian friend stopped by to show Bishop an interesting old necklace. Its tiny red shell beads were strung on sinew, and hanging as pendants were three acorn-sized gold nuggets.

This, said the Indian, came from a cave in the mountains — a cave filled with many more artifacts of the ancient inhabitants of the Mojave Desert.

With the information came a map which "contained landmarks to a small box canyon. Entrance to the canyon was through a rock crevice scarcely wide enough to admit a man. The opening appeared in the side of a rocky ravine. Inside, a shadowy slot cut across the floor of the range. On one wall were petroglyphs . . . On the other wall, high above the floor of the narrow canyon, were the dozen shelter caves."

Two years later, Bishop found the caves — but he could not reach them. The rock wall was shear, and he had no rope to drop down into the openings from above. All he could do was try to peak into the caves. In one he saw (or thought he saw) a piece of matting or a basket.

Bishop never got this close again. All we know is that the tiny canyon is "somewhere in the vicinity of La-motte Springs." Also, Bishop found the 100 - foot - long *cul - de - sac* from above, because a cave-in had covered the yard-wide mouth of the box canyon, which opened into a larger wash.

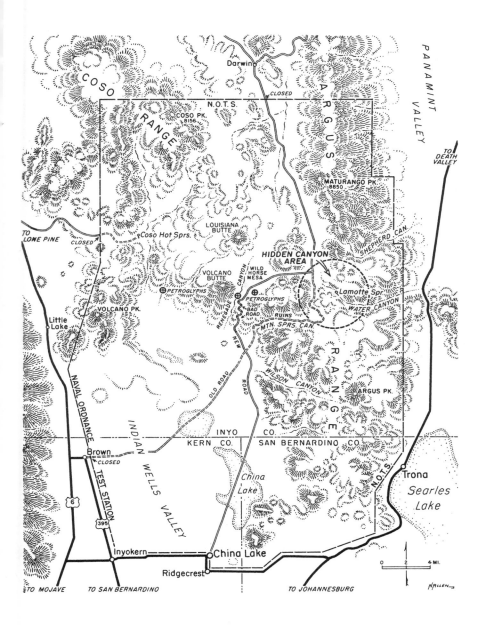

John Nummel Gold

THIS IS THE FIRST of two lost gold mine stories concerning John Nummel (see "John Nummel Silver," page 203). Both are told by Harold O. Weight—the gold tale in the March, 1956, *DESERT*.

Nummel spent his days in the Lower Colorado River country, walking wherever he went — and he went considerable distance and covered much ground, most of it anything but level.

On one such hike — from the Red Cloud Mine to the La Fortuna Mine — Nummel made his strike. There is a disagreement as to the date, but it most likely was just before the turn of the century.

Fifty years later, Nummel described his discovery to Clyde Stewart of Picacho: "It was hot as the devil . . . and there was that paloverde tree. I went over and sat down in its shade. My canteen was pretty near empty, but I took a drink anyway. Then I just sat there and rested in the shade. There was a sort of ledge — looked like dirty quartz — cropping out right beside me where I was sitting . . . It was yellow quartz. And it was rich! And pretty! Free yellow gold . . ."

He continued on to La Fortuna. His plan was to go to work, save up enough money, and then develop the ledge. Too bad. He was never able to find the gold again. Nummel died in 1948.

According to Stewart, the trail between the two mines crossed Yuma Wash about three miles from the Colorado River.

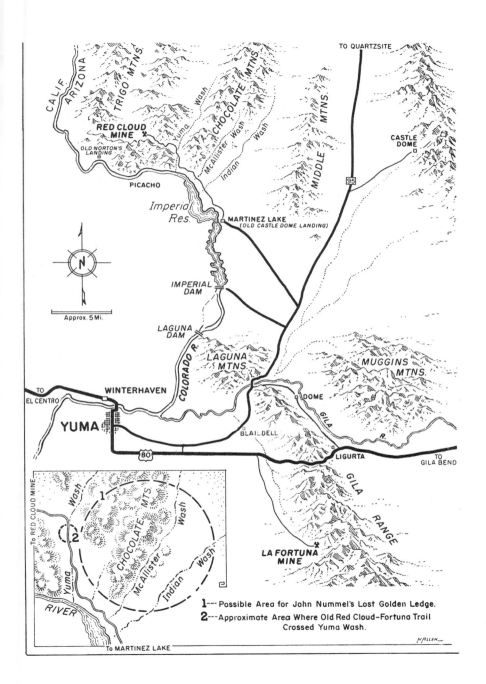

TO QUARTZSITE

CALIF.
ARIZONA

TRIGO MTNS.

CHOCOLATE MTNS.

RED CLOUD
MINE ✗

OLD NORTON'S
LANDING □

MIDDLE MTNS.

CASTLE
DOME

Yuma Wash

McAllister Wash

Indian Wash

PICACHO

Imperial
Res.

MARTINEZ LAKE
(OLD CASTLE DOME LANDING)

95

N

Approx. 5 Mi.

IMPERIAL
DAM

LAGUNA
DAM

COLORADO R.

LAGUNA
MTNS.

MUGGINS
MTNS.

TO
EL CENTRO

WINTERHAVEN

DOME

GILA R.

YUMA

BLAISDELL

80

LIGURTA

TO
GILA BEND

GILA
RANGE

LA FORTUNA
MINE ✗

To RED CLOUD MINE

Wash

Yuma

Wash

1

2

CHOCOLATE MTS.

McAllister

Indian Wash

Wash

RIVER

To MARTINEZ LAKE

1--- Possible Area for John Nummel's Lost Golden Ledge.
2--- Approximate Area Where Old Red Cloud-Fortuna Trail
Crossed Yuma Wash.

N.ALLEN

Gold in Morgan City Wash

In 1934, Palmer C. Ashley was helping his dad work a lowgrade prospect near Morgan City Wash, 23 miles out of Wickenburg, Arizona. He tells the story in the April, 1956, *DESERT*.

The two-man operation was tough work, and so when Ashley's dad had to go into Phoenix on business and he told his son to take it easy, the young man decided to take a ramble to a lead deposit which needed examining.

A passing prospector had told him about it. "I was told," wrote Ashley, "to hike a half-mile up the wash to a 20-foot-high wall on the wash's right bank. This wall had vertical eroded ridges resembling a pipe organ. Over this wall and back of the next rise was a prospect hole with large chunks of galena on the surface."

So off he went, directly to the wash, but was uncertain about the fluted wall. "I climbed the first one I came to and hiked over the first rise, but found no prospect hole."

Ashley retraced his steps to the bank of the wash and continued on. At each intersecting wash, he descended the wash floor to look for the fluted wall.

It was on one of these descents that he stumbled and fell down a rather steep slope, receiving a painful bruise.

As he rested, he noticed "a ledge of pure white quartz streaked with red and green discoloration." He broke off a piece and put it in his sample sack.

Then he stopped for lunch, and in the afternoon climbed another fluted wall and found the lead prospect hole.

Back at the cabin, Ashley, father and son, emptied the sack and studied the lead ore specimens. Then the white, red and green quartz rock caught the older man's attention. His son hastened to add that he had merely thought this rock was pretty, that it would go nicely in the rock garden.

The father "examined the upper surface (of the rock) with his glass and then turned the piece over. We both gasped!" The underside was covered with fine wire gold and pinhead nuggets.

That night the Ashleys went to bed dreaming of riches, but they were never able to retrace the son's path to the ledge.

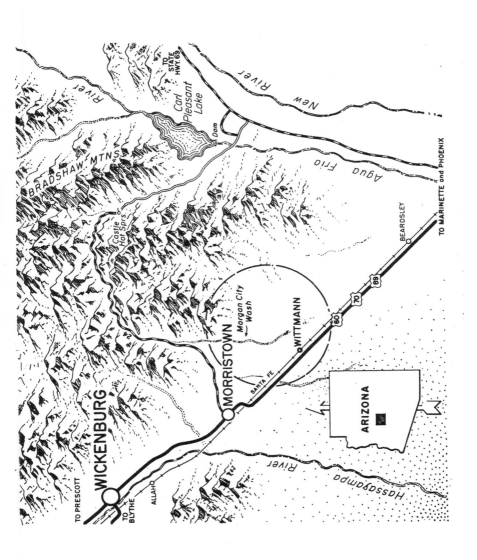

Hank Brandt's Gold

CALIFORNIA'S SUPERSTITION MOUNTAIN lies 15 to 20 airline miles northwest of El Centro. From a distance it looks "like a cloud of smoke," as it was described in a 1929 USGS report. Oldtimers say it's a not-quite dead volcano that gives off fumes, noises and mysterious signs.

Actually it is a quite common ridge of gray biotite granite. The mountain's southwestern face is almost buried by fine quartz sand.

In his October, 1956, *DESERT* report, Harold O. Weight follows the waybill to Hank Brandt's gold, as described in Philip A. Bailey's *Golden Mirages* (published in 1941).

Bailey wrote that Brandt had a secret cache in Superstition from which he took out about $4000 every spring for a period of eight years. Upon his death he left a friend $16,000 in raw and minted gold. He also left directions to the mine, which filtered down to Bailey: "three miles east of Coyote Wells on Highway 80, turn north and cross the washes to a place where jade may be found. From here head for a certain dark-appearing cut in the Superstitions. The course leads northeastward across the old Butterfield route. If you are on the correct route, you will find a place where there are several petrified palm trees and a pile of old whalebones. Continuing on this course, your next landmarks are two dry lakes. The larger one, at the south, has two big ironwoods on its northern edge. This dry lake is known as Dos Mesquites Lake.

"Cross the lake near the trees in such a way that the course is parallel to an imaginary line into the Superstitions. When you have found the correct entrance to the mountain, follow the canyon upward until it reaches a small mesa, and then look for another canyon leading down the eastern front of the mountain. The walls of this second canyon are reddish-brown sandstone. In this canyon a petrified ship will be found. A deep notch where the bow of the ship lay can be seen. Sandstone has formed around the ancient ship, and at present all that remains is the curving line of the ship's beam and some petrified pieces of what was once a very fine-grained wood planking.

"Having located the canyon of the ship, follow it down to its mouth on the eastern front and then turn north along a wall of purple talc between some small hills. After passing the talc stratum, you will find a canyon similar

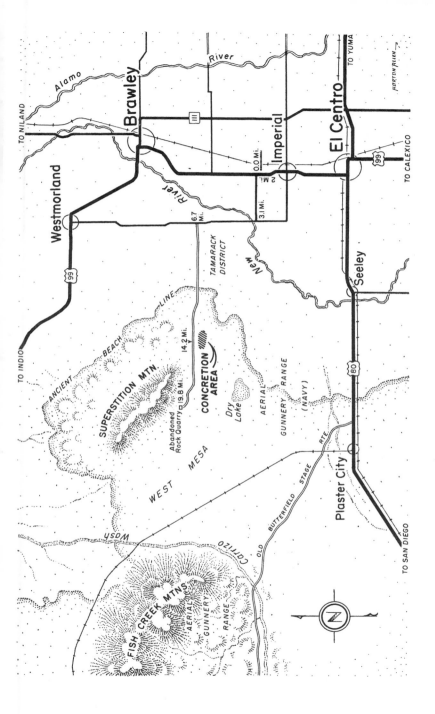

to that containing the ship. This canyon is filled with low, stubby mesquite bushes. You then will come to a high bank out of which a big rock protrudes. Turn the corner of this rock sharply, and you will see a big ocotillo stalk set in the rocks. The mine is above in a hidden gully."

Weight had no trouble finding the "jade". There's not much of this greenish material around, but it is there — "scattered over the desert below Highway 80." (Incidentally, this rock will take a polish and it does have some of the gem qualities of true jade.)

Weight also found the "dark opening into Superstition." (In fact, he found a half-dozen such openings.) The "petrified palm trees" escaped him, but there are many pieces of dark, fine-grained petrified wood in this region.

"As for the whalebones — I have heard more than one person insist that certain concretions are skeletons of prehistoric animals, and we did come upon some which we likened to whalebones," wrote Weight. ". . . I located a reddish sandstone canyon with what I judged were the remains of the petrified ship — a deep notch in the side of the canyon where the bow had rested, a curved area in the sandstone which might mark the beam, and a few fine grained chunks of petrified wood, one of which even looked a bit like planking."

But, here the trail grows cold. Weight confesses in a brave show of honesty — rare in dedicated lost mine hunters — that he gave up the search in favor of going on a field trip for concretions, with which the desert is favored.

Little Horn Gold

JUAN BAUTISTA ALVARADO was a governor of California in Spanish days. His son, Jose Alvarado Sr., migrated to the Gila Valley of Arizona in 1878, where he homesteaded a piece of ground and ran cattle. To his son, Jose Alvarado Jr., he gave directions to a fabulously rich gold strike in the Little Horn Mountains. Jose Jr., told the story to Harold O. Weight, and Weight told it to *DESERT* readers in January, 1957.

When Jose Sr. was running cattle, many Tonto Apaches camped on his land. For the most part, these were friendly Indians, responding with kindness to the many favors, big and little, the Alvarados did for them. The Tonto Apaches were being shuffled back and forth by the Army, and for the homeless Indians these were trying times.

One of the Apaches, a warrior named Pancho, was particularly indebted to Jose Sr. Pancho's child had become ill, and Jose Sr. had taken him to the priest to be baptized, and the papoose recovered.

In Pancho's book, he owed Jose Sr. a favor, and tried to repay it years later.

"I have come to take you to the richest mine in the world," he told the aged and crippled Alvarado. For this the Spaniard left his sickbed.

There were four men in the party — Pancho, Jose Sr., and two of the latter's friends. Unfortunately, the two tag-along Spaniards didn't like Indians. They refused to eat with Pancho — and this didn't set well with the proud redman.

He took Jose Sr. aside and told him he had a mind to kill the two Spaniards, a sure cure for prejudice. One thing for sure: there would be no gold for them. They might just as well go back, for Pancho wasn't going to help those two rats get rich.

So all four men turned for home. The Indian slipped away, on a pretext of hunting wild sheep, and when he returned he had a present for his friend: a rock studded with gold.

And now for directions, landmarks: The party left Palomas, where Jose Sr. lived, and traveled in a northwesterly direction, keeping west of the Palomas and White Tank mountains. Apparently they followed the old

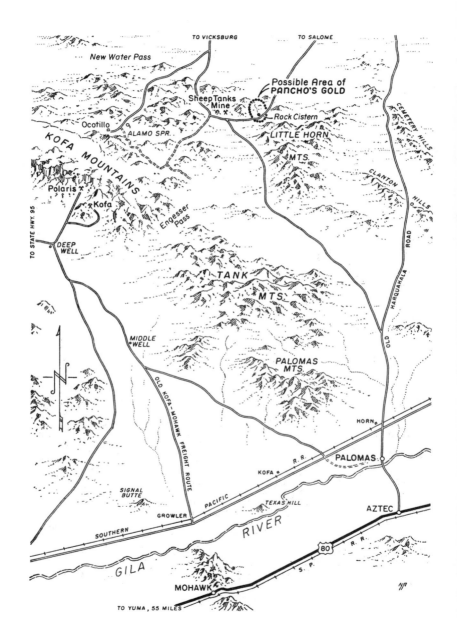

New Water Pass

TO VICKSBURG

TO SALOME

Possible Area of
PANCHO'S GOLD

Sheep Tanks
Mine

Rock Cistern

Ocotillo

ALAMO SPR.

LITTLE HORN

CEMETERY HILLS

KOFA MOUNTAINS

MTS.

CLANTON HILLS

Polaris

Kofa

Engesser
Pass

TO STATE HWY. 95

DEEP
WELL

OLD HARQUAHALA ROAD

TANK

MTS.

MIDDLE
WELL

PALOMAS
MTS.

HORN

OLD KOFA—MOHAWK FREIGHT ROUTE

R.R.

PALOMAS

KOFA

SIGNAL
BUTTE

PACIFIC

TEXAS HILL

AZTEC

SOUTHERN

GROWLER

RIVER

80

S. P.

R.R.

GILA

MOHAWK

TO YUMA, 55 MILES

Yuma Road for a while, then branched north on the freighting road serving the Kofa and Polaris mines. After a few miles they veered east through the Kofa Mountains at Engesser Pass.

About now the Indian was completely fed-up with the two unfriendly Spaniards, and took the party off-course to Alamo Springs in the northeastern outliers of the Kofas.

Next morning he left the group to go "hunting." He gave Jose Sr. these instructions: ". . . you go . . . to the east. You will find a big wash —an old river bed. Below the trail, where it crosses this wash — about 50 yards down — you will find a hole in the rock. The soldiers made it to catch water when the wash runs. Wait there for me."

It was at the camp at the cistern that Pancho brought his friend the rock with a rusty reddish-black surface and golden insides.

Pancho took Jose Sr. aside and gave him explicit directions to the gold source: ". . . go right up this wash a mile and a half to a little side wash. You will see lots of this rock down there. That's the richest mine in the world . . ." Exit Pancho.

A week later (this took place in 1918, according to Jose Jr.) a desperately ill Jose Sr. was brought to Yuma to die. On his deathbed, he told all he knew to his son.

Why didn't Alvarado the Younger go after the gold? He was doing well in the demanding dairy business — he couldn't leave it. Years later, when he did make a try for the gold, the trails were gone or changed. He had no luck.

Enter now author Harold Weight, who not only writes about lost mines, but looks for them, too. During his search he ran across a miner named Ray Hovetter, who was working a dozen manganese claims near the Little Horn Mountains.

Hovetter was a walking storehouse of information.

He knew where the cistern was — just off the old Indian and pack train trail from Alamo Spring.

And Hovetter remembered seeing the elder Alvarado in that country — but he placed the date nearer 1910 than 1918.

And he told of the rich strike Bill and J. V. Allison had made "in a butte at the side of that wash only a few hundred yards from the waterhole. Reddish ore with the gold just sticking out." (The Allisons' vein was shallow, and soon petered out.)

Weight found the cistern — but the gold — if any remains — is still all Pancho's.

The Great Diamond Hoax

SOMEWHERE NORTHEAST OF Vernal there may be diamonds, raw rubies, sapphires and emeralds lying on the ground that could possibly be worth 50 or 100 or even 1000 times their weight in diamonds, raw rubies, sapphires and emeralds, respectively.

Anyone who knows his Western history — and has the money — will gladly pay you a handsome price for the precious stones. They will be worth it, for they were important to the West's most fantastic swindle.

The story has too many ins and outs to detail its every twist. Suffice it to say that two rough miners pulled the wool over some of the country's shrewdest men — including William C. Ralston, head of the Bank of California and financial autocrat of the Pacific Coast. The year was 1872.

The miners, Philip Arnold and John Slack, had salted a small field near where Utah-Colorado-Wyoming come together. Incredibly, the precious stones they used — actually inferior specimens purchased in Europe — bore the rough marks of lapidary tools! And yet the bankers, overcome by the possibility of acquiring great fortune, ignored the tell-tale evidence that these stones had been handled — and rejected — in a jeweler's shop.

Tiffany's of New York appraised the sack of gems Arnold and Slack had brought to Ralston for "safekeeping": $1,500,000! A catastrophic error.

Henry Janin, the nation's leading mine authority at that time, inspected the "mine field" with Slack and Arnold. The party left the Union Pacific Railroad at Rawlings Springs, near what is now Green River, Wyoming. After an erratic four-day trip southward through the wilderness, they reached the area where the two miners had thrust an iron rod into the ground, dropped a few near-worthless stones into the holes, and then filled them over.

This description of the mine field comes to us: "It embraced a small mesa of about 30 or 40 acres at an elevation of 7000 feet. A small stream of water ran through it."

Janin gave the field his unqualified endorsement: "Twenty laborers could wash out a million dollars worth of gems indefinitely."

The San Francisco and New York Mining and Commercial Company

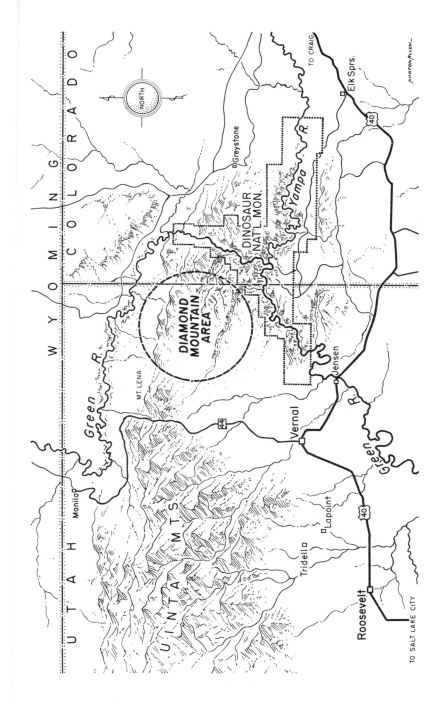

was created. Twenty-five men were "permitted" to subscribe for stock to the amount of $80,000 each. The House of Rothschild was to act as foreign agent.

Slack and Arnold were paid off: $660,000.

A mining engineer, Clarence King, brought everyone back down to earth. He found the field, dug up some gems and made his report.

Slack was never heard from again. Arnold opened a bank in Kentucky (the state refused to extradite the man who had skinned the Yankees) and was killed in a gun fight the following year. Ralston's bank closed its doors three years later, and his body was found floating in the Bay.

DESERT'S February, 1957, story was written by H. N. Ferguson.

Silver in the Trigos

WRITING IN THE MAY, 1957, *DESERT*, Harold O. Weight described the lost silver in the Trigo Mountains north of Yuma as the "most elusive of lost ledges."

It is a story of frustration — several men have been to the ledge. They've described it, practically pinpointed it, and sampled its ore. But, who today can give explicit directions to where it lies baking in the desert sun?

Let's take the discoverers in order:

1. A Mexican prospector whose name is forgotten. He gave rich samples of the ore to Jose Maria Mendivil, prominent Picacho miner-businessman-prospector. The ledge was "within a day's journey" north of the rich Silver Clip Mine. Mendivil was the man who had discovered the Clip, greatest lead-silver producer in the Lower Colorado silver district. In a four-year period (1883-87), the Clip disgorged a million dollars. Mendivil sold the claim for $200.

When Mendivil finally got around to assaying the ore the Mexican had given him, much time had elapsed. The silver values were rich, but the Mexican had left the country.

2. An Indian whose name is forgotten. This man led the mine super-intendent of the Silver Clip to the ledge. The superintendent's name was Pickenbaugh, but everyone called him Pennybaker. He was married to an Indian woman, and the Indian who led him to the ledge north of the Clip probably was a relative.

In those days, when you worked for a salary, as Pennybaker did, the company owned you 24 hours a day. This is one important reason advanced for the fact that Pennybaker did not follow-up on the ledge. Pennybaker went over to the Harquahala when the Clip closed down, and then retired to Los Angeles.

But, the silver ledge began gnawing at his insides, and he returned to the river country. Pennybaker and the late Bert Hart, who had a ranch near Cibola, made an attempt at discovery — and failed. Pennybaker made two, possibly three, more attempts — all failures.

3. Santiago Lopez. The leading cattleman in this area in the late 1880s, Lopez drove his cattle to Yuma via Clip Wash from the river to a point less

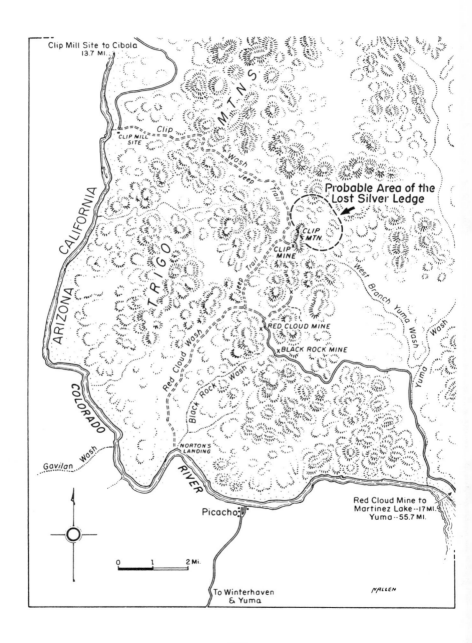

Clip Mill Site to Cibola
13.7 MI.

CALIFORNIA

ARIZONA

CLIP MILL
SITE

Clip

Wash

Jeep

Trail

M.T.N.S.

Probable Area of the
Lost Silver Ledge

CLIP
MTN.

CLIP
MINE

Jeep Trail

West Branch Yuma Wash

Wash

T·R·I·G·O

Red Cloud Wash

Black Rock Wash

Jeep Trail

RED CLOUD MINE

BLACK ROCK MINE

Yuma

COLORADO

Gavilan Wash

NORTON'S
LANDING

RIVER

Picacho

Red Cloud Mine to
Martinez Lake--17 MI.
Yuma--55.7 MI.

0   1   2 Mi.

To Winterhaven
& Yuma

NALLEN

— 190 —

than two miles from the mine, where a left fork entered. "Here the cattle trail took the side wash, went through a pass in low hills just to the north of Clip Mountain and then entered a basin at the head of a west branch of Yuma Wash."

Somewhere in the pass area north of Clip Mountain — on or near the cattle trail — Lopez found the silver ledge. After depositing the cattle in Yuma, he returned quickly as he could — but could not relocate the silver.

4. Julian Parra. Son of Felisario Parra, discoverer of the Mesquite Diggings in the Chocolate Mountains of California, Julian concentrated his mining efforts in the river country. He found the ledge, placed a monument on it, reaffirmed the fact that it was richer than the Clip, reported its location as being along the old trail north of Clip Mountain — but was never able to return to it.

5. Earl Kerr. A latter-day resident of this area, Kerr found "a big silver ledge in just about the right area" in 1951. He made the prospecting trip with George Converse and Sumner Farrar, although Kerr is the only one of the three who saw the ledge and made a grab sample of its ore.

Kerr gave Weight this information: the ledge is "on the contact between the andesite and red granite. You can see it from half a mile away. Going over a saddle, it stands up in the air about four feet, and it's about 15 feet wide and shows up for about 30 feet. I don't think they got in the right district hunting it, because they didn't think there was any ore on that side of the mountain . . ."

Kerr's ore didn't show a good assay, but as he said, it was a grab sample.

A return trip was planned, but Kerr died suddenly.

— 191 —

Gold of the Four Peaks

"Go By Way Of the Bush Highway to the sign that marks the turnoff to Hughes Ranch, then proceed to the Hughes Well. At this point there is a junction of two washes. Take the southerly wash about five miles east. Here there will be evidence of an old digging in the side of the wash. Climb out of the wash onto the bench, and seek the biggest paloverde tree in sight. At the base of the tree measure 20 feet southwest; the opening of the mine is at that point."

Speaking: an 86-year-old Apache named Iretaba, also known as Puncher Bob (because he had been a horse and cow wrangler in central Arizona's Four Peaks area).

Listening: an 80-year-old mining engineer, Colby Thomas.

The gold-rich quartz blowout hole had been discovered by a pair of white men in the mid 1800s. They worked the mine briefly, then were killed by Apaches who apparently didn't like people — especially non-Apaches.

Iretaba's father had been in the party of extermination. He grew up on the story of how papa killed the white miners. He even sneaked over to the blowhole and broke off pieces of the rich quartz. The elders didn't like this and they punished young Iretaba. A boy who wasted his time playing with pretty yellow rocks was capable of all sorts of foolishness — even making friends with non-Apaches.

Iretaba had done exactly that — made friends with Colby Thomas. And now he wanted to do something nice for him — and besides, Iretaba was now the eldest of the elders — and he had knowledge of what that yellow metal could do for a poor blind Indian.

Thomas, despite his age, made a search for the gold, and failed.

He took in a partner, Ed Abbott, and he failed, too. They returned to Mesa to get more details — but Iretaba and his son had vamoosed.

Thomas died in 1952.

The story is told by E. C. Thoroman in the November, 1957, *DESERT*.

———————

THE FOUR PEAKS COUNTRY figures in three other lost mine tales by John D. Mitchell:

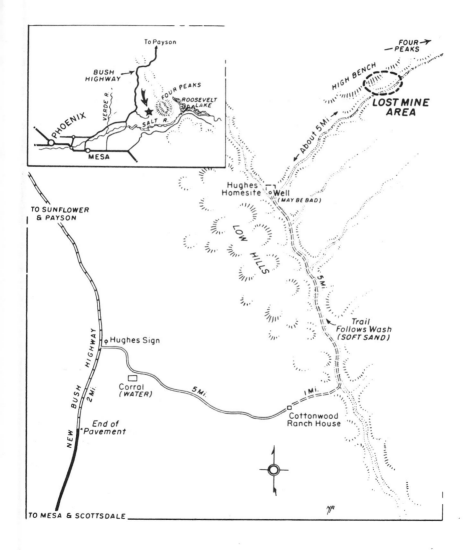

May, 1941 — Lost Pesh-la-chi ("gold mine," according to Mitchell). A Doctor Thorne, Arizona pioneer, is shown a rich ledge of gold by the Tonto Apaches by whom he is held captive. The peek at the gold vein, and release from bondage, are rewards to the doctor for having healed some sick Indians. Unfortunately, the Indians blindfold the doctor before and after he sees the gold — and thus he is never able to reurn to the vein.

September, 1941 — Lost Black Maverick. Cowboy Yaqui Valentino was riding the range in the lower reaches of the Four Peaks. The ground was thick with manzanita and scrub oak, but there was a clearing with a little stream of water. The bull Valentino lassoed chose the puddle of water to land in — and his struggle to regain his footing "scoured the sand off the richest specimen of gold ore the cowboy had ever seen." He never saw it again.

January, 1949 — Lost Squaw Hollow Ledge — Squaw Hollow being "about 40 miles north of Phoenix in the Camp Creek country, and about 10 miles south of Bronco Canyon". In 1864, Apaches chased-out a group of white men who had made a gold strike here.

Papuan's Lost Placer

THE MOHAVE INDIAN, Chinkinnow, always had gold with which to buy supplies from the white traders — gold that came from a concealed digging supposedly in the desert mountains west of Blythe.

Dorothy Robertson wrote the story for *DESERT's* March 1958, issue. Her husband got the details while in Blythe in 1926 — five years after Chinkinnow was last seen in one of the little desert settlements in this area, trading gold for groceries.

Chinkinnow was the adopted son of Papuan, a Papago Indian who had migrated north as a result of Apache troubles. He married an outcast Mohave woman, thus giving her status. In exchange she gave-up her secret: a gold deposit in the McCoy Mountains.

The Indian couple shared their gold with the Mohave camp, and these people did most of their trading at Bill McCoy's government post store at Ehrenberg. (The McCoy Mountains were named after him.)

McCoy accumulated $75,000 worth of these gold nuggets — but he wanted more. He and the other storekeepers tried every trick in the book, but could not pry loose the secret.

Then Papuan went to his reward. Twenty years pass, and into Ehrenberg comes a brawny middle-aged German named Hartmann. He made a concerted effort to win the old woman's friendship — but failed. He did learn from her that Chinkinnow had been let in on the secret and that he was actively mining the placer deposit.

The German tried wooing Chinkinnow — with the same negative results.

Men followed Chinkinnow on his gold-gathering forays, but he always lost them. Some people suggest the deposit is in the Castle Dome Mountains on the opposite side of the river; that Chinkinnow always started off to the west toward the McCoys, then backtracked.

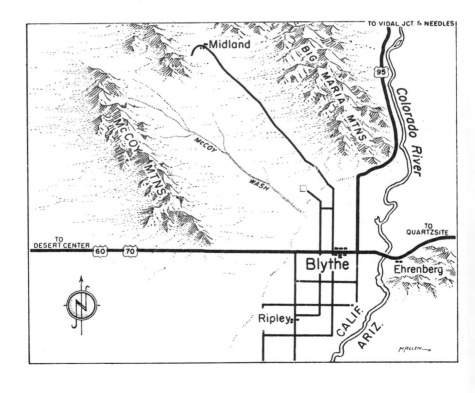

Morrow Turquoise

In 1958, I interviewed four brothers who had "grown up with the hills" of the central Mojave Desert. The Morrows were then living in Oro Grande, but in their younger days had roamed the length and breadth of this region. One of them had been accused of "digging every hole in this country." Mining was in their blood; their dad, who came to California from Missouri in 1857, gave his name to the Morrow Mining District which embraces Slocum Mountain, 26 miles east and slightly south of Randsburg, and 30 miles north and slightly west of Barstow.

When I talked to the Morrow boys in '58, Roy was 85 years of age; Jim, 83; Harry, 77; and Raymond Victor "Penny," 72. Sixty years previously, Roy and Jim had discovered and briefly worked a turquoise mine in the Slocum Mountains. Let the brothers tell the story:

"We were working in Copper City, a good camp a couple of miles north of Slocum Mountain, when we made that Turquoise strike," recalled Roy. "Jim and I were riding by the low ridge on the west slope of the mountain when we spot this outcrop.

"It was eye-level. We dug in about 10 feet under this ledge and blasted another five. All we found were these big turquoise nuggets, but very little copper."

"Turquoise was no account," said Harry.

"It was positively no account," Roy agreed.

"Jimmy," Roy said, "remember how them Indians grabbed up all our turquoise samples?"

Jim chuckled with the memory.

"Yes, there were plenty of Indians in this country then," Roy continued. "They wore lots of this turquoise jewelry.

"Well, we worked this ledge three-four weeks, hauled all this turquoise out, and when we saw it wasn't going to pay, we left it. We wanted copper — not turquoise."

Harry spoke next: "We've tried off and on during all these years. Every

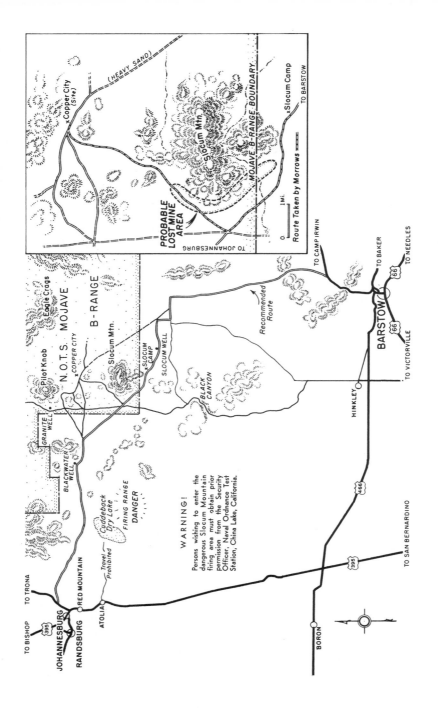

WARNING!

Persons wishing to enter the dangerous Slocum Mountain firing area must obtain prior permission from the Security Officer, Naval Ordnance Test Station, China Lake, California.

time turquoise climbed in market value, we'd try harder — but we couldn't find Jim and Roy's mine. It's a tough lay-out."

The Morrows had last tried in 1955 — and could not even find traces of other old workings in the turquoise mine area. In fact, they could not relocate Slocum Camp at the south tip of the mountain.

"The thing to find is that old wagon trail from Slocum Camp to Copper City we were on when we spotted that outcrop — but that is gone too," said Jim. "Seems to me the mine was in low hills, kind of at the bottom."

"'Nearest I can remember exactly," said Roy, "is that Jim and I were five miles south of Copper City when we found that ledge."

"About that turquoise mine," Penny said, "it's a good one. Turquoise is more valuable than silver today. We'd be looking for it yet if we could get out there, but you go ahead and print the story because now we never will find it. Next time you come to Oro Grande we'll all be up at the cemetery."

The story appeared in the October, 1958, *DESERT*.

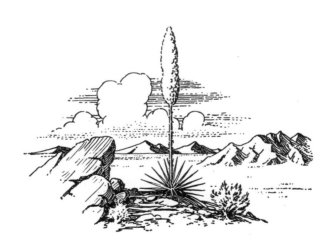

Dutchman's Laguna Gold

THE LATE ED ROCHESTER supplied writer Harold O. Weight with much mining lore. Loved and respected, Rochester is destined to become an important part of the romance of the Desert West.

In Weight's story of the Old Dutchman's lost ledge of gold (*DESERT*, December, 1958), we have still another case of Rochester having seen and examined the ore (in this case he sold three pieces of it at Sanguinetti's Store in Yuma for $62 "and a big black cigar"). Rochester got the facts from the prospector who made the strike. This is unimpeachable data.

The Old Dutchman had a heavy cart and two burros — an outfit that limited his cross-country mobility. And the country he chose to cross — the jumbled complex of mountains in the bow of the Lower Colorado River — is not exactly blessed with good natural cart roads. All this by way of saying there's not too many places the Old Dutchman could have been when he made his strike.

Unfortunately for him, his burros broke into the grub box and ate, or rendered unedible, its contents. And thus the Dutchman had to quit mining and get out — or starve.

He had come into the area by way of the ferry at Picacho. From there he had traveled south, destination Laguna Dam.

"Soon he came to a little basin fairly high up in the hills. From it he could see only one little green spot of Colorado River bottomland . . . He also saw, in a southerly direction, rising smoke which he reasoned came from . . . Laguna Dam. There was a waterhole in the basin, so the Dutchman camped and prospected. And in this vicinity he found his high-grade vein . . ."

And so — thanks to the thoughtless burros — he headed for the smoke at Laguna Dam. But he had not reckoned on steep-walled Senator Wash. There was no way to get his outfit through. He turned east — toward the river.

Rochester was camped on the river. He remembered the year as either 1910 or 1911, before Imperial Dam was built (water backed-up by the dam covers the campsite).

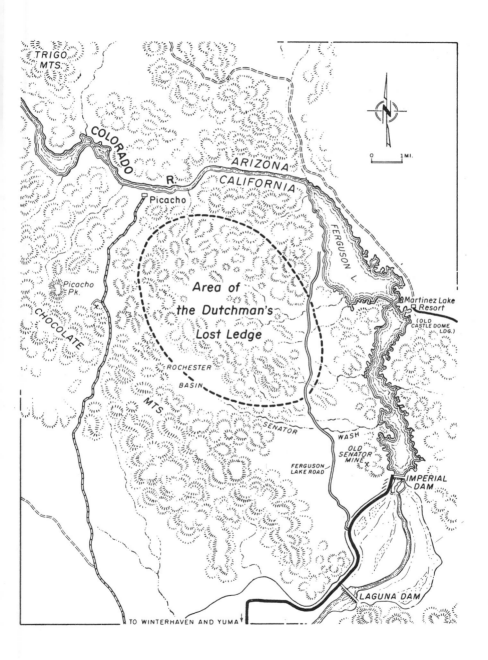

The Dutchman came into Ed's camp, ate his fill, and divulged the facts regarding his strike, as quoted above.

He paid Rochester the three pieces of gold to ferry himself, most of his supplies, and the two animals across the river. He cached the cart.

The Old Dutchman explained that he wanted to return to Quartzsite to pay off his grubstaker, storekeeper William E. Scott, and organize a big effort to develop the rich ledge.

Rochester continued downriver to Yuma and Sanguinetti's Store and the big black cigar. From there he went to Los Angeles.

As it turned out, Rochester was the last man to see the Dutchman alive — at least in that part of the world. When Ed returned to Quartzsite a year later, he learned from storekeeper Scott that the old prospector had not kept his appointment. The cart was still stashed in the arrowweeds on the west bank of the river. The wheel tracks had been erased by the elements.

Rochester found what he believed to be the right basin, complete with waterhole — a 100-acre tract lying north of Rochester Basin. He even found a ledge.

He found everything — except the gold.

John Nummel Silver

JOHN NUMMEL WAS a walker. He had to be — the Trigo Mountains are a long way from even bad roads.

He had a cabin on the Colorado River, a few miles northwest of Norton's Landing, in the late 1920s or early 1930s, reported Harold O. Weight in the April, 1959, *DESERT*. And Nummel had a job as caretaker of the shut-down Red Cloud Mine. There were a lot of rugged miles between.

John made the hike many times — seldom taking the same trail twice (he was a prospector first, a caretaker second).

The silver strike came on a cabin-bound hike from the Red Cloud. He picked-up several samples along the way and dumped them in his yard for a close look — someday.

Walter Riley, a longtime friend and prominent Yuma mining man, looked over the specimens in Nummel's yard, singled out *the* rock and asked John if he could have it assayed.

When the men next met, Riley told his friend the news: the rock was fabulously rich.

Nummel tried — in fact he covered every wash, trail and route he ever remembered walking in the Trigos — but the silver ledge eluded him.

John's native silver could have come from a mine between the Red Cloud and Mohave Tanks operated by a Dutchman. This theory from Jose Alvarado, who knew the Dutchman when he was working at the King of Arizona Mine and Alvarado was working the mill there.

Nummel died at the Pioneers' Home in Prescott in 1948. (See also page 176).

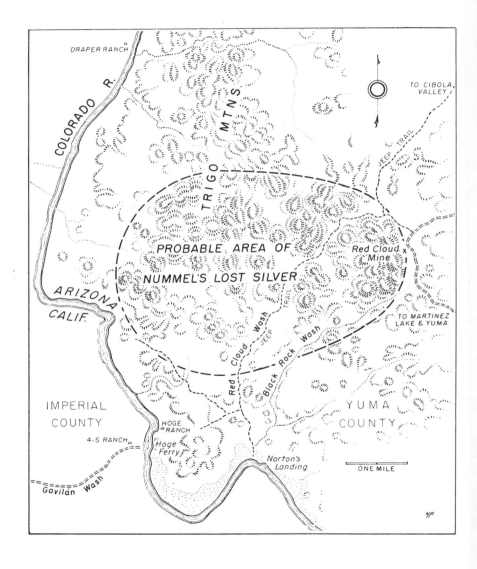

DRAPER RANCH

COLORADO R.

TRIGO MTNS

TO CIBOLA VALLEY

JEEP TRAIL

PROBABLE AREA OF
NUMMEL'S LOST SILVER

Red Cloud x
Mine

ARIZONA
CALIF.

Red Cloud Wash

JEEP TRAIL

Black Rock Wash

TO MARTINEZ
LAKE & YUMA

IMPERIAL
COUNTY

4-S RANCH

HOGE
RANCH

Hoge
Ferry

Norton's
Landing

YUMA
COUNTY

ONE MILE

Gavilan Wash

NP

Alec Ramy's Bonanza

HE LOST THE GOLD, but gained his life. For this exchange, Alec Ramy, sheepherder and prospector, was eternally grateful. But, this is not to say that he was willing to abandon the search.

In 1904, Ramy was prospecting the southern portion of the Last Chance Range in the Death Valley environs. One night his burros broke away from the dry camp and headed "directly across the salt-encrusted flatlands to the base of the distant Inyo Mountains."

Ramy was wise in the ways of the desert. He knew it would have been suicide to strike out across the valley to recover the animals. Instead, he decided to move on to an area of sand tanks "several miles south along the foothills." These tanks were natural catch-basins for water, and at that particular moment Ramy needed water more than he did mules — or gold.

He reached the tanks late that afternoon. His feet were badly blistered. But, there was worse news: the tanks were dry.

And now the question of life or death was squarely up to Ramy's bleeding feet. On he went — southward. During the nightmare which followed, he "stumbled over a protruding quartz ledge. It contained particles of gold plainly visible to the naked eye. It was a bonanza!"

The old prospector was saved by a band of Indians. Later, he told his story to a Maritime Alps countryman, a sheepman named Alfred Giraud. The tale was "illustrated" with rich samples of gold from the ledge.

Time — and Ramy — pass. Fifty years later, Giraud cleans out his attic and finds a chunk of Ramy's gold. It assays 50 percent gold — one of the richest pieces of ore ever found in this part of California.

Giraud takes the Ramy lost mine seriously and begins his investigation. At Isabella, he meets a Chilean named Crisante Santavinas, who carries around the same story — and an identical piece of Ramy gold! They exchange notes, sift facts.

Giraud makes still one more amazing discovery. He meets the ancient Indian woman, Stina Duck, wife of Grapevine Duck, who had cut the shoes from Ramy's bleeding feet at his rescue.

At the time Ken Wortley's story appeared in *DESERT's* May, 1959, issue, Giraud was back at his Bishop ranch, preparing for an expedition to the Ramy treasure.

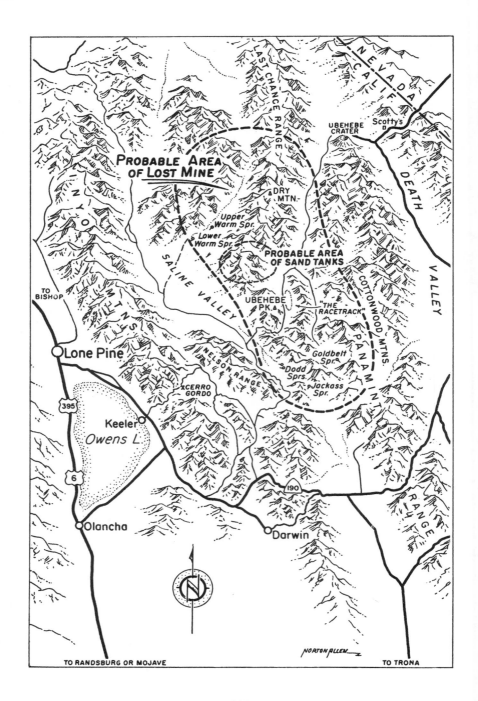

PROBABLE AREA
of LOST MINE

PROBABLE AREA
OF SAND TANKS

NEVADA
CALIF

UBEHEBE
CRATER

Scotty's

DEATH

VALLEY

DRY
MTN.

Upper
Warm Spr.

Lower
Warm Spr.

INYO

LAST CHANCE RANGE

SALINE VALLEY

TO
BISHOP

UBEHEBE
PK.

"THE
RACETRACK"

COTTONWOOD MTNS.

PANAMINT

Lone Pine

NELSON RANGE

Goldbelt
Spr.

Dodd
Sprs.

Jackass
Spr.

XCERRO
GORDO

395

Keeler

Owens L.

6

RANGE

190

Olancha

Darwin

N

NORTON ALLEN

TO RANDSBURG OR MOJAVE

TO TRONA

Papago Arsenal

PROSPECTOR W. E. BANCROFT, who came to Arizona in 1874, stumbled on a base metal treasure probably worth double its weight in gold. The metal was fashioned into guns — "Old Queen Anns, old Yawgers, old Hawkins, all kinds of old flint-locks, both shot guns and rifles, and . . . at least 100 different makes of pistols. There must have been at least 1000!"

Bancroft found the cache on the Papago Indian Reservation in 1882. He said he was on a prospecting trip from Casa Grande to Covered Wells. ". . . he was passing through the Santa Rosa Valley on his way south to his claims (at Covered Wells), when he noticed some odd-looking rock formations several miles to the west. He decided to inspect the promising mineral area, and several days later, while climbing in among the outcrop, spotted a rectangular adobe building . . . 40 to 50 feet long and 15 to 25 feet wide . . ."

He broke into the structure and there discovered the Papago arsenal. "I saw guns in there," he wrote in a 1926 newspaper article, "that I think Cortez had when he invaded Mexico or Coronado might have brought them to this country . . ." *DESERT's* story, written by anthropologist Bernard L. Fontana, was released in January, 1960.

Franciscan Father Bonaventure Oblasser, leading authority on the Papagos, told Fontana that he had never heard of a weapon arsenal — but thinks there is a good chance one exists. In the late 1870s, the Pimas and Papagos were having trouble with white settlers along the Gila River. Traditionally, the Papagos cached their weapons near the positions of potential enemies.

Permission to search Papago lands must be obtained from the tribal council (Sells, Arizona). The searcher must agree beforehand to turn over the guns to the Tribe.

———————

A SIMILAR ARSENAL, this one a stockpile of Paiute arrows in a cave near Pyramid Lake in northcentral Nevada, is reported by Perry G. Powers (*DESERT*, May, 1960). The arrow cave is on the northeast side of Pyramid.

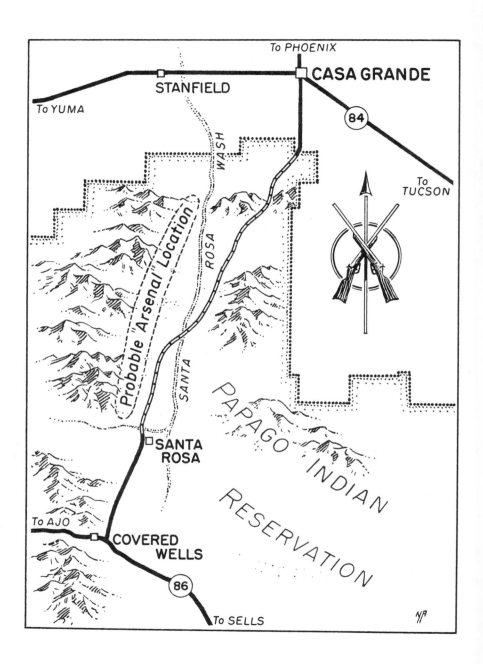

Wilson's Lost Mine

HIS NAME WAS Jonathan W. Wilson, but he was known in Mojave Desert mining circles as Quartz, Chuckawalla, Johnny, Charley and Dirty-Shirt Wilson.

He operated out of the Twentynine Palms oasis in the 1880s. His mining career was highlighted by discoveries of the Virginia Dale Mine east of Twentynine Palms, and the El Dorado on the edge of Pinto Basin, now within the boundaries of Joshua Tree National Monument.

Also connected to his good name (s) is the matter of the Lost Wilson Silver Mine, described in the May, 1960, *DESERT*, by Harold O. Weight.

Some people infer that Wilson's brain had cooked too long in the desert sun. The San Bernardino *Index* told its readers that the mine was "a base fabrication manufactured out of whole cloth."

Laugh at old Dirty-Shirt, despise his habit of overselling a mine; but what of the horn silver ore he showed around San Bernardino? It came from somewhere. Wilson said that pinpoint on the desert was between the Providence and the Old Woman mountains.

His starting point was "a little spring in the Providences." Fortunately for wildlife, but unfortunately for the lost mine hunters, there are many springs in this disjointed mountain mass.

Darkness caught Wilson far from his goal and out of water. It was cold and windy. The old prospector gathered loose rocks and made a half-moon shelter.

At daybreak he discovered that his building material was "immensely rich horn silver."

The assay pegged the value of the ore at $15,000 to the ton. It earned Wilson four partners, all prominent San Bernardino County men, well-known in the mining world of the 1880s.

And then — confusion. The group split-up after the search failed. But in the fall of 1885, one of the partners, Hank Brown, rediscovered — and promptly re-lost — the Wilson bonanza.

Weight wonders if Wilson might not have obtained his silver sample from the great Bonanza King Mine in the Providence Mountains. We will never know.

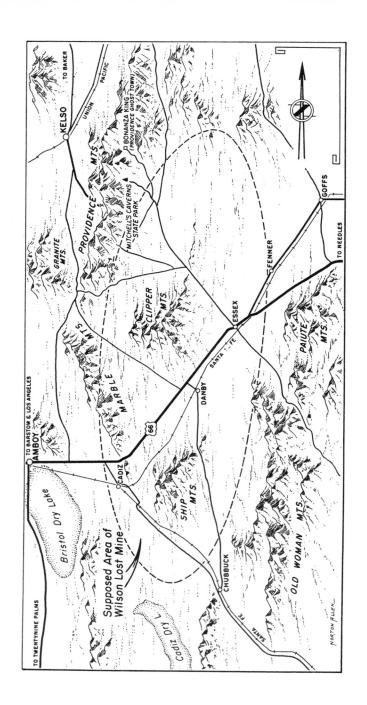

TO BAKER

KELSO

UNION PACIFIC

PROVIDENCE MTS.

BONANZA KING
(PROVIDENCE GHOST TOWN)

MITCHELL'S CAVERNS
STATE PARK

GRANITE MTS.

GOFFS

TO NEEDLES

FENNER

CLIPPER MTS.

ESSEX

SANTA FE

MARBLE MTS.

PAIUTE MTS.

DANBY

66

TO BARSTOW & LOS ANGELES

AMBOY

CADIZ

SHIP MTS.

OLD WOMAN MTS.

Bristol Dry Lake

Supposed Area of
Wilson Lost Mine

CHUBBUCK

SANTA FE

TO TWENTYNINE PALMS

Cadiz Dry

NORTON ALLEN

The Sands of La Posa

THE MAP TELLS the story. In the 1880s, the owner of the Planet Mine was in Ehrenberg, on the Colorado River. To return to his mine, logically he should have followed the river road north to where the town of Parker stands today, then cut east through the Buckskin Mountains. Or he could have gone due east from Ehrenberg on the Fort Whipple road to Desert Well, then north on the Bill Williams River freighting road. Harold O. Weight reports on the Planet man's lost gold in the February, 1961, *DESERT*.

Our hero took an original route back to his mine. "I got drunk," he reportedly said, ". . . it was pretty hot. I didn't have any water . . . I came by the Marquita Mine. Then I could see Planet Mountain. I headed for Planet Mountain."

La Posa Plain provided relatively easy going at first, but then the miner " . . . got into sand. A lot of dunes. Finally I came to a low black hill surrounded by sand . . . I got off my horse and rested awhile."

Despite his serious situation, he was a prospector first, last and always. He picked-up some of the heavy black rocks at his feet, and placed them in the saddle bag. ". . . I got back on my horse . . . and that was the last I remembered." The horse continued on.

Enter now Sam Butler and his brother, who had left the Harquahala Mine "for a little excitement and lubricating" at Ehrenberg.

They met the now riderless horse in Bouse Valley, recognized it, and back-tracked its trail. The Butlers hauled the unconscious Planet Mine owner to Ehrenberg.

He did not live long, but his brother made a routine assay of the black ore — it went $750 to the ton in gold, silver and copper. Needless to say, the subsequent attempts to find the black hill were failures.

Harold Weight's story is based on information given him by William G. Keiser of Quartzsite. Keiser, in turn, got his facts directly from Sam Butler at Bouse, in 1908.

There are two other versions of this story.

1). The strike was made in the 1870s by a prospector "attempting a

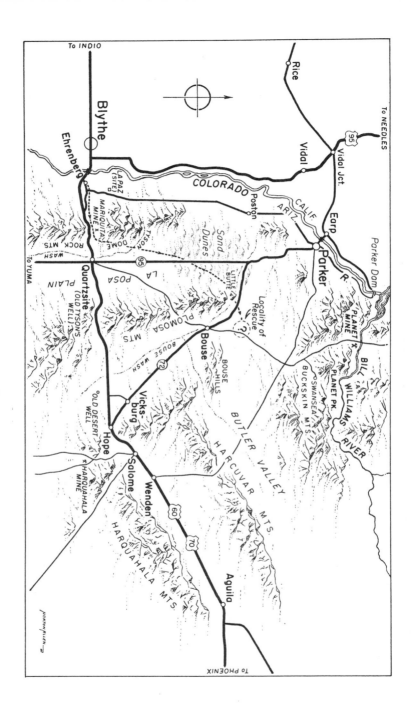

To INDIO

Rice

To NEEDLES

Blythe

Vidal

Vidal Jct.

95

Ehrenberg

COLORADO

Poston

CALIF.

ARIZ.

Parker R.

Earp

Parker

Parker Dam

LA PAZ
(SITE)

MARIQUITA
MINE ✕

TYSON DOME

ROCK MTS.

Sand
Dunes

WASH

To YUMA

Quartzsite
(OLD TYSON'S
WELL)

95

LA POSA

PLAIN

LITTLE
BUTTE

PLOMOSA MTS.

Locality of
Rescue

PLANET
MINE ✕

✕ PLANET PK.

BILL WILLIAMS RIVER

BUCKSKIN MTS.

SWANSEA ✕

Bouse

72

BOUSE WASH

BOUSE
HILLS

BUTLER VALLEY

"OLD DESERT
WELL"

Vicks-
burg

HARCUVAR MTS.

Hope

Salome

✕ HARQUAHALA
MINE

Wenden

60

70

HARQUAHALA MTS.

Aguila

NORTON ELLEN

To PHOENIX

direct crossing from Tyson's Well (Quartzsite) to the Planet Mine." His ore assayed $750 to the ton.

2). John Mitchell's "Lost Sixshooter" yarn concerns itself with the Planet owner "getting lost in a sandstorm on the way home (from Quartzsite), seeking shelter beside a ledge and finding it rich in free gold." This was $25,000-per-ton ore.

THE HARQUAHALA MOUNTAINS area is the setting of the Frenchman's Lost Gold legend, as reported in the October, 1942, *DESERT*, by John D. Mitchell.

The year was 1867. Two Frenchmen brought-in $8000-plus in "rough gold," and deposited it at the W. B. Hooper and Co. store in Yuma. Then they disappeared. In '73, Apache-fighter King Woolsey found a large pile of rich ore on a "well-marked trail through the Tenhachape Pass."

A. H. Peeples (of Rich Hill fame) said that he saw three Frenchmen working a prospect in the Harquahala country in 1868.

Sullivan's Gold

THE PRINCIPAL CHARACTER in this store is an Irishman named Jim Sullivan, floor manager of Billy Horan's Stingaree Saloon at Hedges (Tumco) in the Cargo-Muchacho Mountains. Horan related Sullivan's tale of woe to the late Ed Rochester who in turn passed it on to Harold O. Weight. The latter's story was in the June, 1961, *DESERT*.

Being a bouncer in a tough mining town dive was a demanding job, and apparently Sullivan was well equipped for this sort of work. The gold in his life came from a Christianized Mission Indian who was the Stingaree's swamper.

After much coaxing and persuading, the Indian agreed to lead Sullivan to the place from whence came the nugget samples he had in his possession. Unfortunately for both men, Sullivan's coaxing and persuading job had taken all winter, and now it was summer.

The Irish-Indian team hitched a ride with Horan to the latter's blacksmith shop (another Horan enterprise) on the east flank of the Cargo Muchachos. From there the Indian and Sullivan headed east — perhaps traveling less than 15 miles.

They found the gold ledge, worked it briefly, then returned to base camp.

This wasn't the sort of work Sullivan was used to doing, and he had built-up a mighty thirst. Their water supply consisted of two five-gallon kerosene cans packed-in on a burro. The poor Indian may have known plenty about gold, but he didn't know too much about kerosene cans. He had not cleaned them before filling with water — and Sullivan took a big swig, spat out the water, and pulled out his six-shooters.

Perhaps — for the purposes of recovering lost gold — he would have been better off had he shot the Indian. Instead, he peppered the cans. The tainted water sank into the sand and Sullivan and his partner had no choice but to hike out of the hills or die of thirst.

When they got back to civilization, the Irishman was in bad shape (he had worn low dress shoes). He had to be shipped-out of the rough camp for medical care and rest.

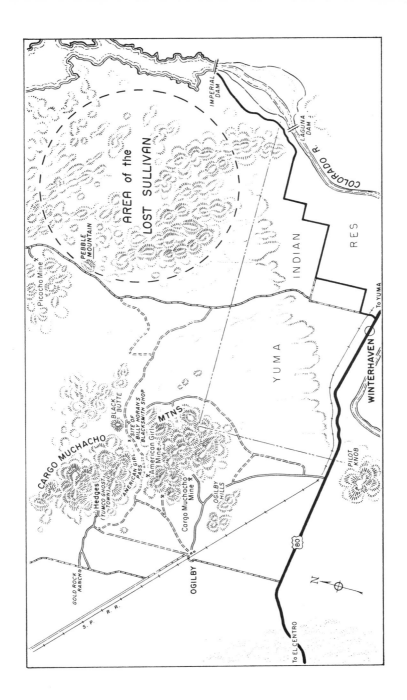

AREA of the
LOST SULLIVAN

PEBBLE
MOUNTAIN

Picacho Mine

IMPERIAL
DAM

LAGUNA
DAM

COLORADO R.

INDIAN

RES

YUMA

To YUMA

WINTERHAVEN

BLACK BUTTE

CARGO MUCHACHO MTNS.

X SITE OF
BILLY MORAN'S
BLACKSMITH SHOP

Hedges
(TUMCO GHOST
TOWN)

AMERICAN GIRL
PASS

American Girl
Mine

Cargo Muchacho
Mine

OGILBY
HILLS

PILOT
KNOB

GOLD ROCK
RANCH

OGILBY

80

S. P. R. R.

N

To EL CENTRO

Monte Cristo Gold

HAROLD O. WEIGHT, writing in the July, 1961, *DESERT*, gets his facts directly from two men — Fred and Logan Gilbert — who spent the greater part of their lives in and around the target area.

In fact, Fred Gilbert saw the $86,000 gold ore which Charles Lampson found near Crow Spring. Although only six years of age at the time, Fred never forgot the rock — clear quartz crowded with gold nuggets strung together with golden threads. That eight-pounder looked like "head cheese," he recalled.

Lampson found the specimen while on a prospecting trip. He made a concerted effort to trace the float, but with no luck. When forced to abandon the enterprise, he told the father of the Gilbert brothers: "You are my friends. I'd rather have you find it than anyone else. You go to San Antone station. Old Man Bell at San Antone will point out Crow Springs to you. It's about 30 miles away, due west. When you get to Crow Springs, go to that little hill about 3½ miles southeast. I picked up this ore right on the saddle of that hill. But I couldn't find any more. I've panned all around it and couldn't find a color."

The elder Gilbert followed Lampson's directions, easily found the hill, but the only values he was able to pan — a low $7 to the ton — were in silver, not gold. While searching for Lampson's gold, he and a partner discovered the Carrie silver-lead mine in the Monte Cristos. This was in 1897.

In 1918, the young Gilbert brothers and a friend joined the search. ". . . about a mile from Crow Spring on a little reddish-pink quartz hill with twin peaks" they found an old location monument. The notice was dated June 6, 1896, and was signed by Charles Lampson and his brother-in-law, Owen Owens.

The following year, Lampson, now an old man, turned up in Tonopah.

The Gilbert boys quickly ushered him to Crow Spring. Lampson took one look at the twin peaks and said, "this is the spot!" Fred showed him the old monument.

Remember — Lampson had told the elder Gilbert that his discovery

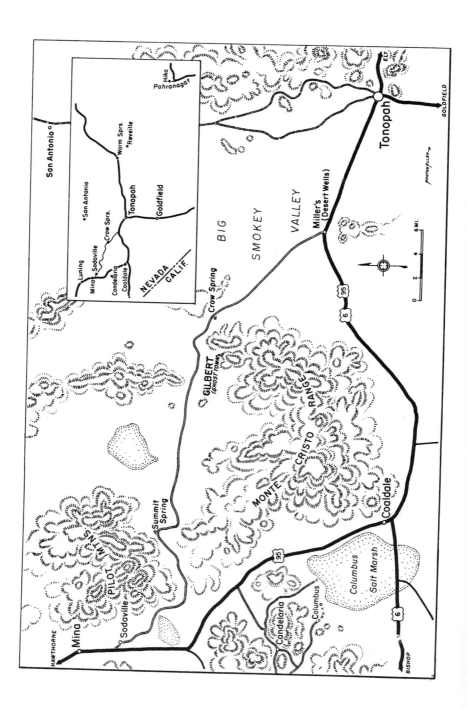

was made "3½ miles southeast of Crow Spring." Now he pointed to ground that was right next to the waterhole.

Apparently, concluded Weight, Lampson was confused when he first told the elder Gilbert how far his strike was from the spring. Also, Crow Spring is southwest — not due west — of San Antonio; and closer to 20 than 30 miles distant.

In September, 1924, the Gilberts — Fred, Logan and a third brother Herman — made the gold discovery in these mountains that resulted in the short-lived town named after the family — Gilbert.

Was it Lampson's gold? No, say the Gilberts. The two ores are entirely different in character. The Gilbert brothers believe Lampson's gold was dropped by a passing Indian at the place where he later found it. But, if this is so, where did the Indian get it?

The Jesuit Answer

WHEN SPAIN'S CARLOS III banished the Society of Jesus from the New World in 1767, he set the stage for a collection of "lost Jesuit treasure" tales which grow bolder and broader with the passing years.

In this book there are several accounts of treasure the Jesuits supposedly buried or hid when the 1767 edict reached their ears — La Purisima Concepcion, Lost Guadalupe, Lost San Pedro, Padre LaRue's Gold, Bells of Guevavi, Lost Treasure of Del Bac, Opata Silver, The Mine With the Iron Door, Carreta Canyon Treasure, Lost Treasure of Sonoyta, Lost Bells of Tumacacori.

"A scholar once said," wrote Jesuit priest Charles W. Polzer in the August, 1962, *DESERT*, "that lost mines and mission-myths are the literary genre of the Southwest. Unwittingly the Spanish colonials picked up the Cibola fever from the Indians and passed it on in new garb. I for one enjoy the tales as a literary form because I believe they capture the haunting reality of an inexplicable country. But taken seriously they are as harmful to history as Jonah in the whale."

In one of *DESERT's* most memorable — and valuable — articles, Fr. Polzer went on to give a "more scientific answer . . . to the perennial doubts raised by" the persistent desert country tales of lost Jesuit treasure:

Physically, Jesuits had access to gold, silver and pearls. Pfeffekorn in his *Description of Sonora* mentions five mines near his mission of Cucurpe. But in his treatment, as in similar works of other missionary padres, it is clear that all the mines were worked by Spanish colonists; many of these men "buried their wealth again" by digging too deeply into unprofitable veins — the age old saga of mining. Segesser mentions a 150-*arroba* (3500-pound) lump of silver discovered near Mission Guevavi; he adds that this meant nothing —"my treasure is souls." Jacob Baegert opines in his *Observations in Lower California* that very little gold was prevalent; the peninsula mines were silver-bearing and these were, at best, mediocre prospects.

Pearls have always been the story-stopper. Everyone thinks of gold and silver — but what of pearls? From the earliest excursions to the *Isla California* the Spanish Crown was vitally interested in developing the pearl fields. Padre

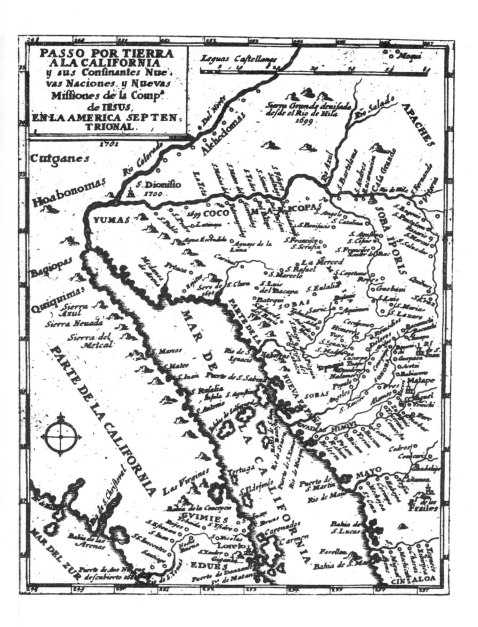

PASSO POR TIERRA
A LA CALIFORNIA
y sus Confinantes Nue-
vas Naciones, y Nuevas
Missiones de la Comp.ª
de IESUS,
EN LA AMERICA SEPTEN-
TRIONAL.

Leguas Castellanas

Cutganes

Hoabonomas

Rio Colorado

S. Dionisio
1700

YUMAS

Bagiopas

Quiquimas

Sierra
Azul
Sierra Neuada
Sierra del
Metcal

Del Norte

Akhodomas

1701

Sierra Grande derniſada
deſde el Rio de Hila
1699

Rio Salado

APACHES

SOBA IPORIS

COCO
MARICOPAS

MAR DE

PARTE DE LA

NUEVA

SOBAS

GUADIAS HUQVI

MATAPE

MAYO

PARTE DE LA CALIFORNIA

La Virgines
Tortuga

EVIMIES

Lorelo

EDUES

MAR DEL ZUR

Puerto de Aus N.
descubierto

CARMEN

Bahia de
S. Lucas

Bahia de S.

CINALOA

— 221 —

Kino's reports on the pearl fishing indicate early disappointment, but some optimism; Atondo was disgruntled at the expedition's paltry pearl profit. And gruff old Padre Baegert, 80 years wiser, put it well:

If a Spaniard after six or eight weeks of fear and hope, sweat and misery, has a net profit of one hundred American pesos, he thinks this is a rare fortune which does not come to all of them, or every year . . .

When the Jesuits moved into the mission frontier, it was not long before their superiors realized the "fabulous wealth of Nueva Viscaya" was going to be a source of trouble between colonization and Christianization. The Society strictly forbade her men to engage in mining or mining affiliated activities in any way. From archival sources we know of only two instances in which Padres became involved in mining operations (these being in the Sierra Madre mission area). In both cases the men were severely reprimanded and removed.

Curiously enough, many people are unaware that the missionaries were not alone on the frontier; that the terrain was dotted with *reals,* commonly centered on colonial mines. In repeated instances the Jesuits refused to perform *any* services for the Spanish colonials in strict obedience to the mining restrictions! This reluctance and later the "anti-slavery" cedula combined to create ill feelings between the missionaires and the colonists . . .

The pearl problem on the peninsula was similar. Spanish vice-regal authority was so intensely concerned over pearl "production," the missionaries went to extreme lengths to avoid conflict with the government . . .

True, in the very early years pearls were used, even set in sacred vessels. But, they became of such a great price they almost cost the whole mission effort.

Preposterous rumors rumbled through Europe that the Jesuits were planning a *coup d'etat,* financed by the gold, silver, and pearls of New Spain! . . .

Mission inventories and details of common practices reveal that little money was kept on hand. So common was credit-buying on the Sonora frontier that the 9% interest and the *quinto* levied on the rough silver cut the purchasing value of available silver and gold. The Padres primarily did not have much money . . .

If any Jesuit treasure has survived, it is physically possible that it is a cache of vestments, sacred vessels, and church ornaments . . .

Mission archives tell us nothing about any cache which was lost after protective burial or concealment during an imminent Indian raid. There are occasional references to this practice, but in each case the missionaires have returned to recover the sacred articles; or the hiding place was discovered by the marauders and the valuables stolen. In no instance were these ever left unrecovered in any church! . . .

Since the majority of the treasure legends hinge on the events of the Society's expulsion in 1767 rather than on Indian raids, the truth or falsity of "hiding the hoard from the Franciscans" depends on a knowledge of the circumstances . . .

On June 24, 1767, the highest authorities in New Spain witnessed the unsealing of the "top secret" orders from Carlos III. Under penalty of death, the orders demanded that within 24 hours each and every Jesuit was to be seized and sent to Vera Cruz, on to Spain, and banishment from the realm. No mean feat for the 18th Century!

In Mexico City that same night 3000 troops, foot and horse, surrounded religious houses. In five residences 178 Jesuits slept unaware of their iron-handed fate. At 4 a.m. the units swarmed through the houses to route the drowsy fathers and brothers to their chapels . . .

Detachments of troops impounded books, sealed records . . . And a note for the treasure seeker: the wealth of the house was confiscated for the royal treasury — 80 pesos cash and an outstanding debt of $40,000. *Net profit:* —$39,920!

The Colegio Espiritu Santo at Puebla was ransacked: floors torn up, walls smashed, toilets searched, and graves opened. Nothing. At the Casa Professa, 100 soldiers invaded the "elite" residence . . .

The searchers, infuriated at the poverty, confiscated the chalices and ciboria. Morning dawned in silence . . . No one could speak . . . to a Jesuit on penalty of death . . .

The same sealed decree with the threat of succeed or die had left the capital posthaste before the sudden suppression of June 25. District military captains lost little time in moving against the Jesuits of the frontier. Sudden and swift secrecy was imperative lest the Indians prevent the plan . . .

The pattern for the frontier demanded that the Jesuits gather at a single mission station in each district. The pretext for the gathering was simply a written order from the religious superior and the voiced purpose of "a great work for the king." While Spanish authority feared the power of these men of God, they did

rely on their unquestioning obedience. Unaware of the true purpose, mission superiors summoned their distant missioners to the rectorates. Each summons was delivered by small detachments of soldiers under the same death threat to clap the Padre in chains and return him under armed guard to the central mission.

Again, records were seized; property confiscated; searches perpetrated; and inventories logged . . .

Distant Sonora and Sinaloa did not hear the decree until July 25 when the 52 Jesuits of the northwest met in the cordoned church of the Colegio San Jose del Matape. Loaded muskets poked through windows and stamping cavalry kicked up plaza dust while Carlos III expelled his civilization-makers from the foremost frontier.

Of all the Mexican Jesuits banished, these men of Sonora suffered most. They were marched to Guaymas in September; eight months were passed in near-shelterless imprisonment in the swampy delta of the Yaqui. They embarked in May, 1768, only to be blown across to California where Portola, after 15 days and the pleas of the Franciscans, permitted the boat load of dying Jesuits to come ashore. Just short of recovery, they sailed for San Blas— driven by Portola's fear of Galvez' impending visit to Loreto. The march across Mexico mimicked the best Bataan tradition, with 20 dropping dead along the route to Guadalajara.

The Padres of the peninsula fared better. While detachments arrested mainland blackrobes, an embargo was clamped on communications with California. For six months no one sailed until Captain Gaspar de Portola landed at San Bernabe, November 30, 1767. His small force crossed the country to seize silver mines, vast agricultural stores, and well organized pueblos. Instead, they clopped across barren hills, passed leathery miners scratching out their lives in hot, dry canyons, and searched for water to quench their thirst.

Word crept up the peninsula in advance of Portola. Padre Ducrue, mission rector, hurried to Loreto to meet the new governor of California. The familiar sequence was repeated; all the missionaries gathered at Loreto and awaited passage for San Blas. Not all was quiet, however; 2000 Indians rioted as San Francisco Borja when Padre Link was removed. But at San Ignatio the neophytes of Padre Retz fashioned a litter to convey him 100 miles to Loreto and exile. Disease, short supplies, universal poverty and the experience of the military captain of California finally convinced Portola that California was not a cornucopia. The peninsula was not a Jesuit heartland empire, but only a desolate mission dependent on Jesuit dedication . . .

What of the gray-robed side of this adventure — the Franciscans? What meager contact occurred in the exchange of the missions demonstrates only kindness and concern. Appeals for the acceptance of the Franciscans were made by the departing Jesuits to their Christian communities; urgent, inadequate attempts were made to impart the languages. As the Franciscans came into complete control, epidemics destroyed whole missions. Records, vestments and ornaments were transferred, many being shipped to Alta, California. Fray Francisco Palou cautiously records these transferrals expressly to prevent charges of mismanagement or loss. Apparently the tide of disbelief on the mainland was beginning to flow against the sons of Francis . . .

Repeatedly Jesuit historians have been asked if there is any truth to the treasure tales. Fr. Peter M. Dunne, S.J., once confided that in his long years of manuscript research no single reference to concealed wealth or a "lost mission" ever turned up. Fr. Ernest Burrus, S. J., the Society's specialist on Spanish colonial history, shudders when he hears the mere mention of the myth. His daily fare is taken amid those "private, secret files" of the Society in Rome. Meticulously he has covered the inventories of the Mexican missions to familiarize himself with authentic Jesuitica. Never has he found any reference to treasure or lost missions. Poverty prevails over the peso.

No doubt precious relics of the mission era remain undiscovered or unrecognized today. But they will be found in forgotten mountain strongholds of Indians long since dead or still superstitious. More likely they will turn up in attics and basements all over the world. We cannot forget the waves of "explorers" who looted the lonely missions, or the "legal" plunder that came with secularization, or the devout protection given by the people against desecration. Some things have found their way back to the churches; some never will. But of the vanished wealth, at least we know nothing was buried or concealed in the missions themselves, and no trail-weary Jesuit ever "lost" his mission. Can you imagine a "Padre Pegleg?"

Real mysteries remain. Where are Eusebio Kino's astrolabe and diary? Keller's notes, and Salvatierra's documents? These are real treasures that lie somewhere in dusty oblivion . . .

A Miser's Fortune

No One, It Seems, had a kind word for Jim Pogue, "the rich miser of Pogue's Station," an outpost on the Nevada desert south of Eureka.

In addition to being miserly, he was distrustful, monopolistic, crooked, and unwashed. He also was rich. — his income was estimated at $25,000 a year.

The money was gained from selling water and feed to passing horses and freight and passenger teams. Pogue's Station boasted a strategic well, and old man Pogue sold his water for as stiff a price as the customer could bear.

The money rolled in — but none of it left the station. No one in the area ever remembers Pogue going away on a trip; he was never robbed; he never banked his cash; he spent money only on tobacco.

Pogue died on May 15, 1915. Three days later the county gave him a *free* burial. By this time the automobile had come to stay, and the horse-watering business was dead, too.

Two years later, a group of men from Duckwater dug up the station yard and found a few coins. More treasure hunters arrived. They tore out one of the station's adobe walls and dug more potholes in the desert.

In 1936, a prospector named John Hoyt found a box containing $11.

Was the miserable human being whom society had ridiculed and shunned, having a laugh from his grave?

Pogue's story is told by Duane G. Newcomb in the November, 1962, *DESERT*.

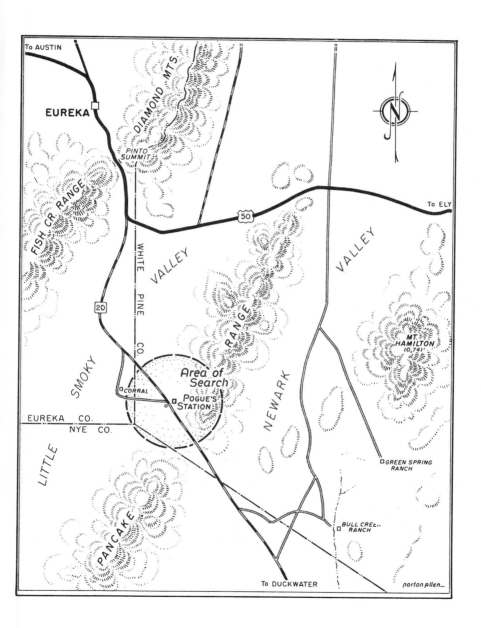

To AUSTIN

EUREKA

DIAMOND MTS.

PINTO SUMMIT

FISH CR. RANGE

WHITE PINE CO.

VALLEY

50

To ELY

20

RANGE

VALLEY

MT. HAMILTON 10,741'

Area of Search

CORRAL

POGUE'S STATION

SMOKY

NEWARK

EUREKA CO.
NYE CO.

LITTLE

PANCAKE

GREEN SPRING RANCH

BULL CREEK RANCH

To DUCKWATER

norton allen

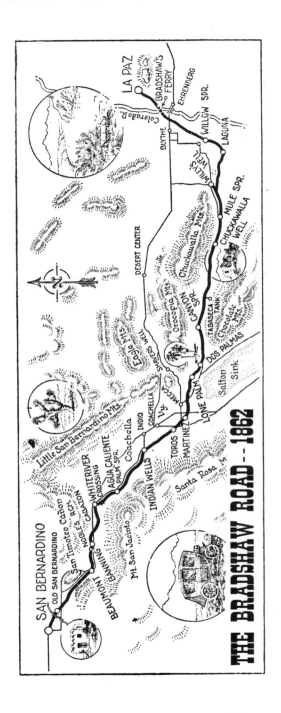

THE BRADSHAW ROAD -- 1862

Trails,
Routes,
Etc.

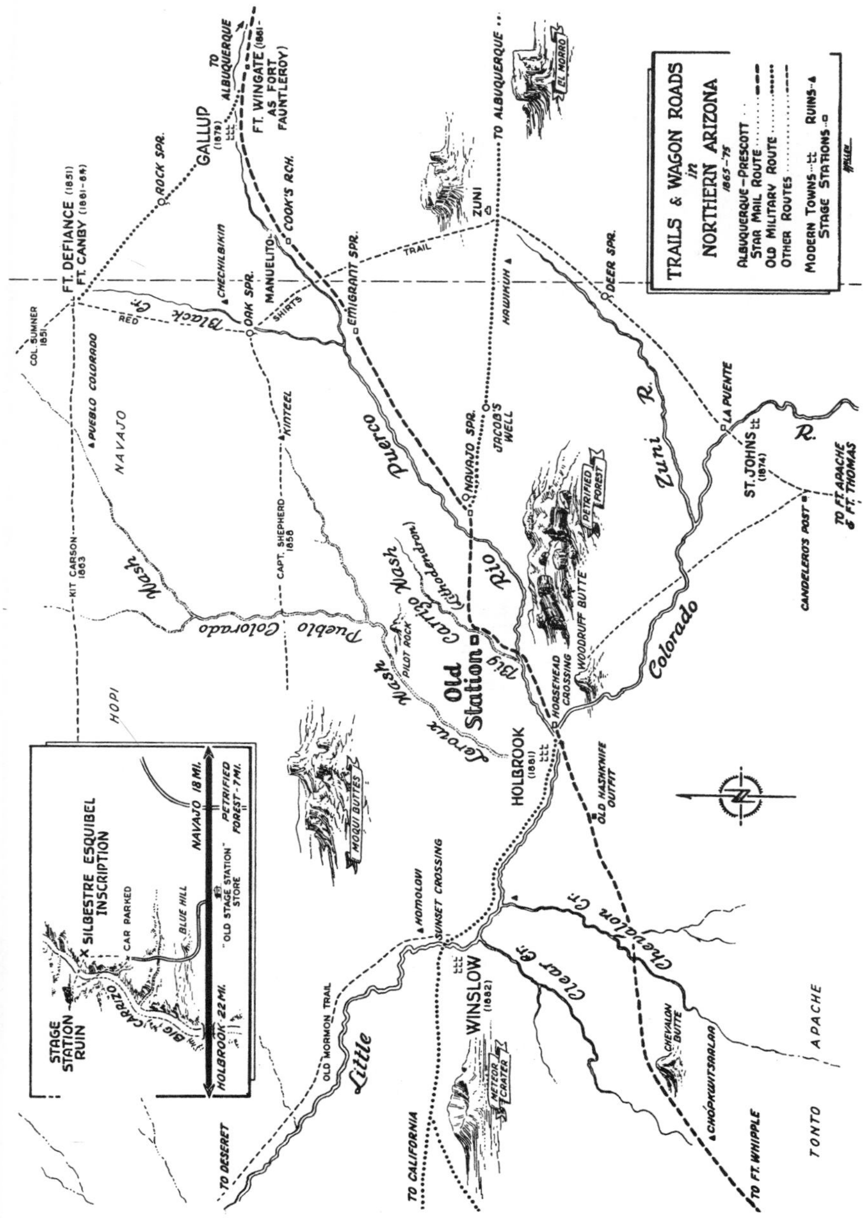

TRAILS & WAGON ROADS in NORTHERN ARIZONA 1865–'75
ALBUQUERQUE–PRESCOTT STAR MAIL ROUTE
OLD MILITARY ROUTE
OTHER ROUTES
MODERN TOWNS
RUINS
STAGE STATIONS
STAGE STATION RUIN
SILBESTRE ESQUIBEL INSCRIPTION
CAR PARKED
BLUE HILL
"OLD STAGE STATION" STORE
HOLBROOK-22 MI.
NAVAJO 18 MI.
PETRIFIED FOREST-7 MI.
BIG CARRIZO
FT. DEFIANCE (1851)
FT. CANBY (1861-64)
COL. SUMNER 1851
KIT CARSON 1863
CAPT. SHEPHERD 1858
ROCK SPR.
GALLUP (1879)
TO ALBUQUERQUE
FT. WINGATE (1861) AS FORT FAUNTLEROY)
COOK'S RCH.
MANUELITO
CHECHILBIKIN
OAK SPR.
RED
SHIRTS
EMIGRANT SPR.
TRAIL
ZUNI
TO ALBUQUERQUE
EL MORRO
HAWIKUH
DEER SPR.
Black Cr.
PUEBLO COLORADO
NAVAJO
KINTEEL
Puerco
NAVAJO SPR.
JACOB'S WELL
PETRIFIED FOREST
Zuni R.
LA PUENTE
ST. JOHNS (1874)
R.
TO FT. APACHE & FT. THOMAS
CANDELERO'S POST
Wash
Pueblo Colorado
Carrizo Wash (Lithodendron)
Rio
PILOT ROCK
Old Station
Big
WOODRUFF BUTTE
HORSEHEAD CROSSING
Colorado
HOPI
Leroux Wash
HOLBROOK (1881)
OLD HASHKNIFE OUTFIT
MOQUI BUTTES
HOMOLOVI
SUNSET CROSSING
Chevelon Cr.
WINSLOW (1882)
Clear Cr.
OLD MORMON TRAIL
Little
METEOR CRATER
CHEVALON BUTTE
CHÓPKWITSARLAA
APACHE
TONTO
TO DESERET
TO CALIFORNIA
TO FT. WHIPPLE

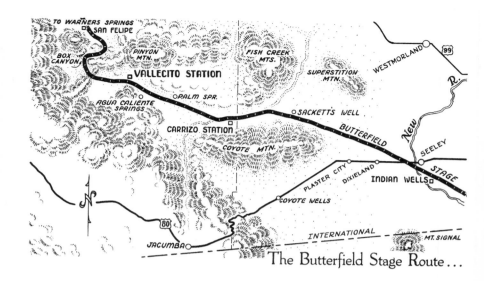

The Butterfield Stage Route...

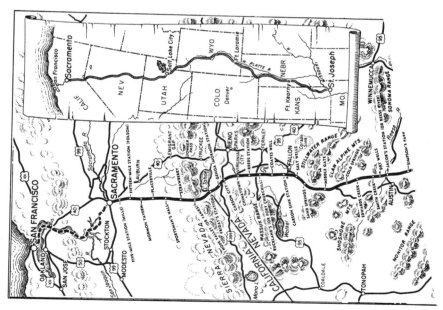

1860-61--The Pony Express Route...

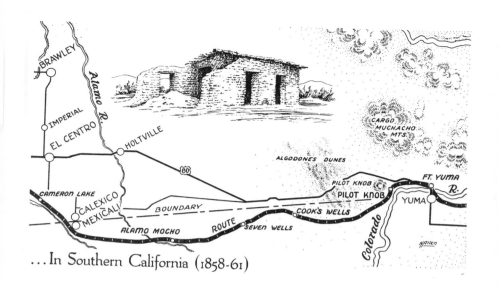

...In Southern California (1858-61)

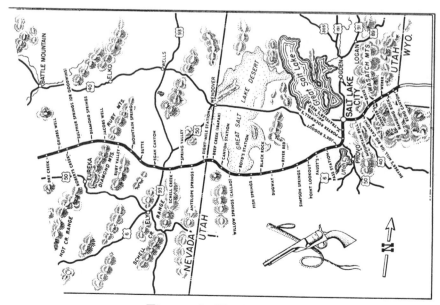

... Through Utah, Nevada and California

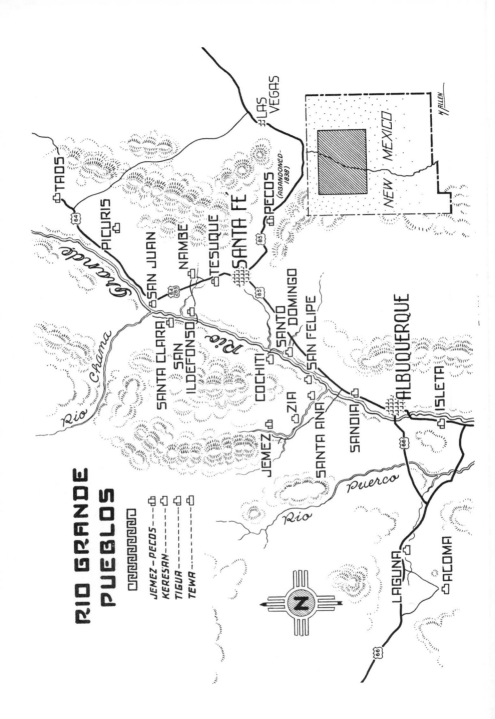

RIO GRANDE PUEBLOS

JEMEZ – PECOS
KERESAN
TIGUA
TEWA

TAOS

PICURIS

Rio Grande

SAN JUAN

NAMBE

SANTA CLARA

SAN ILDEFONSO

Rio Chama

Rio

Rio

TESUQUE

SANTA FE

LAS VEGAS

PECOS
(ABANDONED 1838)

NEW MEXICO

SANTO DOMINGO

COCHITI

ZIA

JEMEZ

SAN FELIPE

SANTA ANA

SANDIA

ALBUQUERQUE

ISLETA

Rio Puerco

Rio

LAGUNA

ACOMA

Z

M. ALLEN

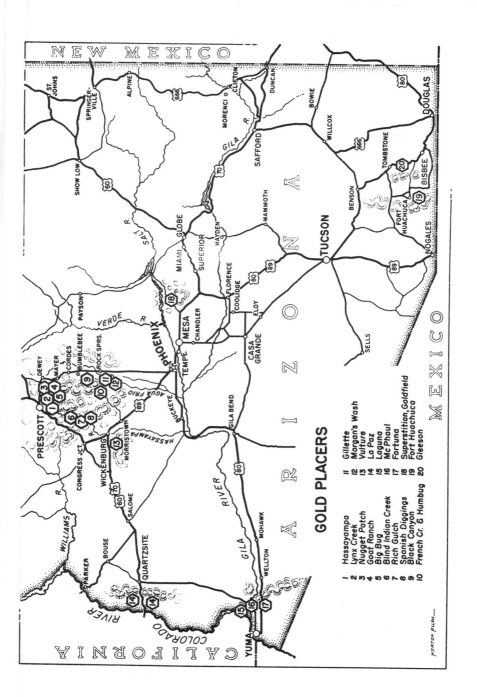

GOLD PLACERS

1 Hassayampa
2 Lynx Creek
3 Nugget Patch
4 Goat Ranch
5 Big Bug
6 Blind Indian Creek
7 Rich Gulch
8 Spanish Diggings
9 Black Canyon
10 French Gr. & Humbug

11 Gillette
12 Morgan's Wash
13 Vulture
14 La Paz
15 Laguna
16 Mc Phaul
17 Fortuna
18 Superstition, Goldfield
19 Fort Huachuca
20 Gleeson

NORTON ALLEN

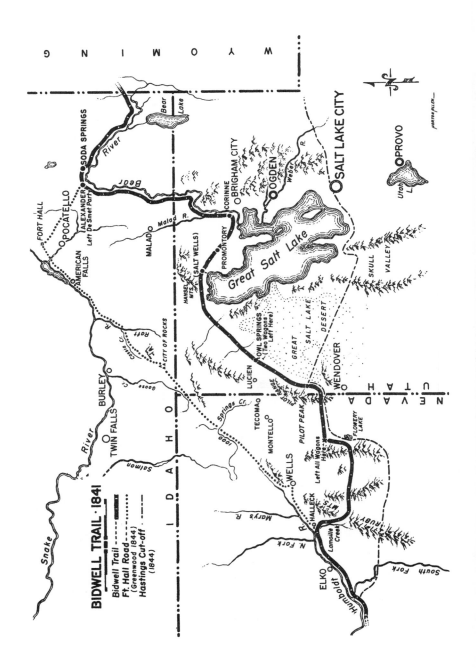

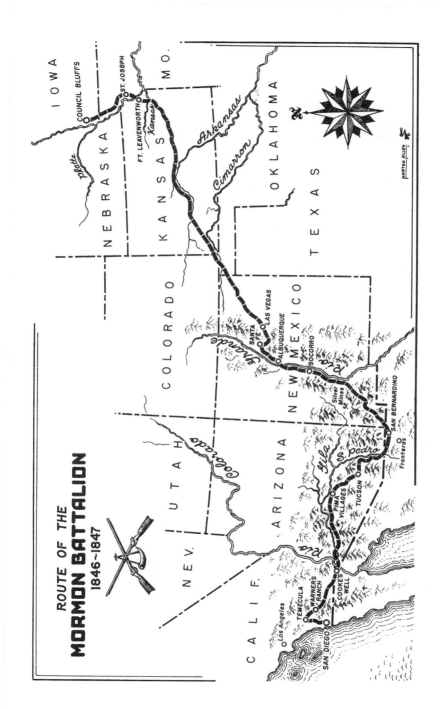

ROUTE OF THE
MORMON BATTALION
1846~1847

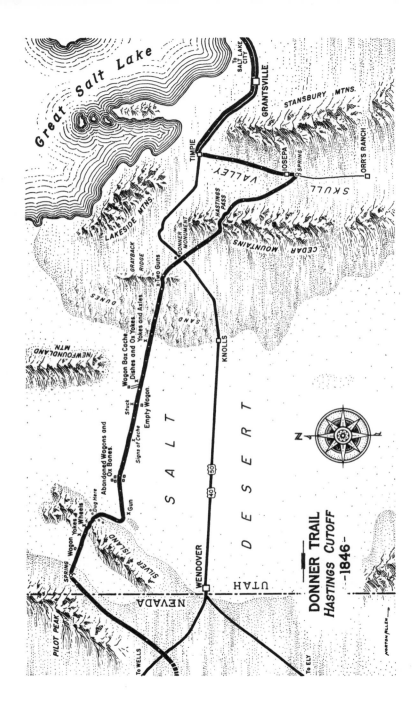

DONNER TRAIL
HASTINGS CUTOFF
--1846--

NORTON ALLEN

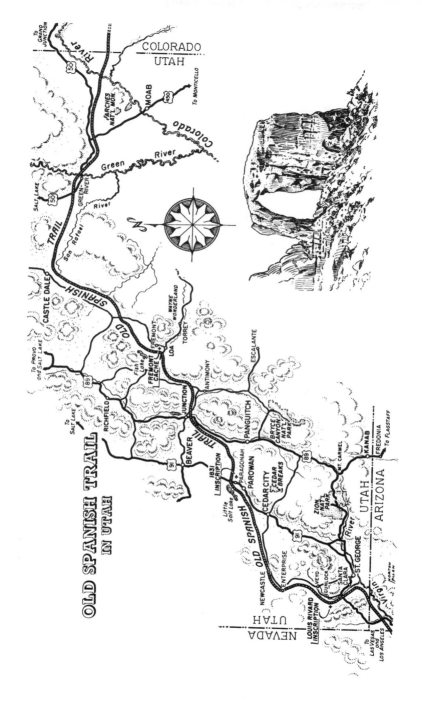

OLD SPANISH TRAIL IN UTAH

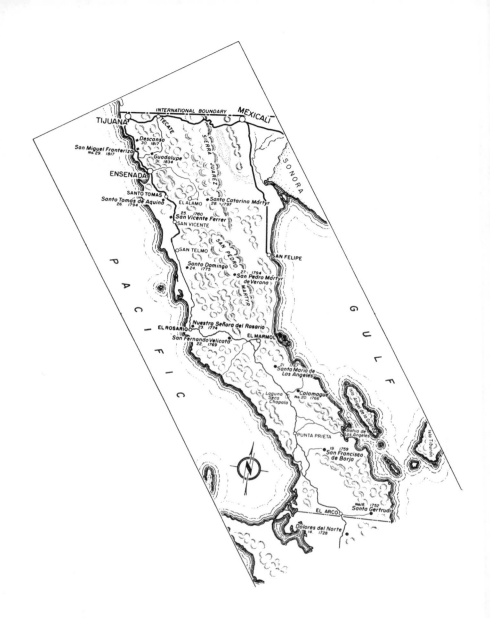

INTERNATIONAL BOUNDARY

MEXICALI

TIJUANA

San Miguel Fronteriza
No. 29. 1817

Descanso
30. 1817

Guadalupe
31. 1834

SIERRA JUAREZ

SONORA

ENSENADA

SANTO TOMAS

Santo Tomas de Aquino
26. 1794

EL ALAMO

Santa Catarina Martyr
28. 1797

25. 1780
San Vicente Ferrer

SAN VICENTE

SAN TELMO

SAN PEDRO

SAN FELIPE

Santo Domingo
24. 1775

27. 1794
San Pedro Martyr
de Verona

MARTIR

PACIFIC

Nuestra Señora del Rosario
23. 1774

EL ROSARIO

San Fernando Velicata
22. 1769

EL MARMOL

21. 1767
Santa Maria de
Los Angeles

Laguna
Seca
Chapala

Calamague
No. 20. 1766

PUNTA PRIETA

Bahia de
Los Angeles

Isla Angel de la Guarda

Isla Tiburon

GULF

19. 1759
San Francisco
de Borja

No.18. 1752
Santa Gertrudis

EL ARCO

Dolores del Norte
14. 1728

— 238 —

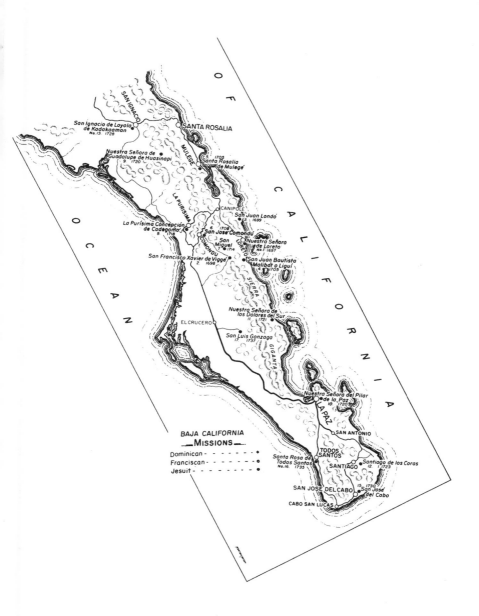

O F

SAN IGNACIO

San Ignacio de Loyola
de Kadakaaman
No. 13. 1728

CALIFORNIA

○ SANTA ROSALIA

MULEGE

Nuestra Señora de
Guadalupe de Huasinapi
9. 1720

1705
Santa Rosalia
de Mulege

LA PURISIMA

● CANIPOLE

San Juan Londo
1. 1699

La Purísima Concepción
de Cadegomó
8. 1718

6   1708
●San Jose Comondu

COMONDU

COMON

San
Miguel
5. 1714

Nuestra Señora
de Loreto
No.1. 1697

San Francisco Xavier de Vigge
2. 1698

San Juan Bautista
Malibat o Ligui
1705

SIERRA

Nuestra Señora de
los Dolores del Sur
11. 1721

EL CRUCERO ○

GIGANTA

San Luis Gonzaga
17. 1737

O C E A N

Nuestra Señora del Pilar
de la Paz
10. 1720

LA PAZ

C A L I F O R N I A

BAJA CALIFORNIA
— MISSIONS —

Dominican - - - - - - - +
Franciscan - - - - - - - ●
Jesuit - - - - - - - - ○

○ SAN ANTONIO

TODOS
SANTOS ○

Santa Rosa de
Todos Santos
No.16. 1735

SANTIAGO ○

Santiago de los Coras
12. 1723

SAN JOSE DEL CABO

15 1730
San Jose
del Cabo

CABO SAN LUCAS

Index

A CATALOG OF SELECTED DOVER
BOOKS IN ALL FIELDS OF INTEREST

CONCERNING THE SPIRITUAL IN ART, Wassily Kandinsky. Pioneering work by father of abstract art. Thoughts on color theory, nature of art. Analysis of earlier masters. 12 illustrations. 80pp. of text. 5⅜ × 8½. 23411-8 Pa. $3.95

ANIMALS: 1,419 Copyright-Free Illustrations of Mammals, Birds, Fish, Insects, etc., Jim Harter (ed.). Clear wood engravings present, in extremely lifelike poses, over 1,000 species of animals. One of the most extensive pictorial sourcebooks of its kind. Captions. Index. 284pp. 9 × 12. 23766-4 Pa. $12.95

CELTIC ART: The Methods of Construction, George Bain. Simple geometric techniques for making Celtic interlacements, spirals, Kells-type initials, animals, humans, etc. Over 500 illustrations. 160pp. 9 × 12. (USO) 22923-8 Pa. $9.95

AN ATLAS OF ANATOMY FOR ARTISTS, Fritz Schider. Most thorough reference work on art anatomy in the world. Hundreds of illustrations, including selections from works by Vesalius, Leonardo, Goya, Ingres, Michelangelo, others. 593 illustrations. 192pp. 7⅛ × 10¼. 20241-0 Pa. $9.95

CELTIC HAND STROKE-BY-STROKE (Irish Half-Uncial from "The Book of Kells"): An Arthur Baker Calligraphy Manual, Arthur Baker. Complete guide to creating each letter of the alphabet in distinctive Celtic manner. Covers hand position, strokes, pens, inks, paper, more. Illustrated. 48pp. 8¼ × 11.
24336-2 Pa. $3.95

EASY ORIGAMI, John Montroll. Charming collection of 32 projects (hat, cup, pelican, piano, swan, many more) specially designed for the novice origami hobbyist. Clearly illustrated easy-to-follow instructions insure that even beginning papercrafters will achieve successful results. 48pp. 8¼ × 11. 27298-2 Pa. $2.95

THE COMPLETE BOOK OF BIRDHOUSE CONSTRUCTION FOR WOOD-WORKERS, Scott D. Campbell. Detailed instructions, illustrations, tables. Also data on bird habitat and instinct patterns. Bibliography. 3 tables. 63 illustrations in 15 figures. 48pp. 5¼ × 8½. 24407-5 Pa. $1.95

BLOOMINGDALE'S ILLUSTRATED 1886 CATALOG: Fashions, Dry Goods and Housewares, Bloomingdale Brothers. Famed merchants' extremely rare catalog depicting about 1,700 products: clothing, housewares, firearms, dry goods, jewelry, more. Invaluable for dating, identifying vintage items. Also, copyright-free graphics for artists, designers. Co-published with Henry Ford Museum & Green-field Village. 160pp. 8¼ × 11. 25780-0 Pa. $9.95

HISTORIC COSTUME IN PICTURES, Braun & Schneider. Over 1,450 costumed figures in clearly detailed engravings—from dawn of civilization to end of 19th century. Captions. Many folk costumes. 256pp. 8⅜ × 11¾. 23150-X Pa. $11.95

CATALOG OF DOVER BOOKS

STICKLEY CRAFTSMAN FURNITURE CATALOGS, Gustav Stickley and L. & J. G. Stickley. Beautiful, functional furniture in two authentic catalogs from 1910. 594 illustrations, including 277 photos, show settles, rockers, armchairs, reclining chairs, bookcases, desks, tables. 183pp. 6½ × 9¼. 23838-5 Pa. $9.95

AMERICAN LOCOMOTIVES IN HISTORIC PHOTOGRAPHS: 1858 to 1949, Ron Ziel (ed.). A rare collection of 126 meticulously detailed official photographs, called "builder portraits," of American locomotives that majestically chronicle the rise of steam locomotive power in America. Introduction. Detailed captions. xi + 129pp. 9 × 12. 27393-8 Pa. $12.95

AMERICA'S LIGHTHOUSES: An Illustrated History, Francis Ross Holland, Jr. Delightfully written, profusely illustrated fact-filled survey of over 200 American lighthouses since 1716. History, anecdotes, technological advances, more. 240pp. 8 × 10¾. 25576-X Pa. $11.95

TOWARDS A NEW ARCHITECTURE, Le Corbusier. Pioneering manifesto by founder of "International School." Technical and aesthetic theories, views of industry, economics, relation of form to function, "mass-production split" and much more. Profusely illustrated. 320pp. 6⅛ × 9¼. (USO) 25023-7 Pa. $9.95

HOW THE OTHER HALF LIVES, Jacob Riis. Famous journalistic record, exposing poverty and degradation of New York slums around 1900, by major social reformer. 100 striking and influential photographs. 233pp. 10 × 7⅞.
22012-5 Pa $10.95

FRUIT KEY AND TWIG KEY TO TREES AND SHRUBS, William M. Harlow. One of the handiest and most widely used identification aids. Fruit key covers 120 deciduous and evergreen species; twig key 160 deciduous species. Easily used. Over 300 photographs. 126pp. 5⅜ × 8½. 20511-8 Pa. $3.95

COMMON BIRD SONGS, Dr. Donald J. Borror. Songs of 60 most common U.S. birds: robins, sparrows, cardinals, bluejays, finches, more—arranged in order of increasing complexity. Up to 9 variations of songs of each species.
Cassette and manual 99911-4 $8.95

ORCHIDS AS HOUSE PLANTS, Rebecca Tyson Northen. Grow cattleyas and many other kinds of orchids—in a window, in a case, or under artificial light. 63 illustrations. 148pp. 5⅜ × 8½. 23261-1 Pa. $4.95

MONSTER MAZES, Dave Phillips. Masterful mazes at four levels of difficulty. Avoid deadly perils and evil creatures to find magical treasures. Solutions for all 32 exciting illustrated puzzles. 48pp. 8¼ × 11. 26005-4 Pa. $2.95

MOZART'S DON GIOVANNI (DOVER OPERA LIBRETTO SERIES), Wolfgang Amadeus Mozart. Introduced and translated by Ellen H. Bleiler. Standard Italian libretto, with complete English translation. Convenient and thoroughly portable—an ideal companion for reading along with a recording or the performance itself. Introduction. List of characters. Plot summary. 121pp. 5¼ × 8½.
24944-1 Pa. $2.95

TECHNICAL MANUAL AND DICTIONARY OF CLASSICAL BALLET, Gail Grant. Defines, explains, comments on steps, movements, poses and concepts. 15-page pictorial section. Basic book for student, viewer. 127pp. 5⅜ × 8½.
21843-0 Pa. $4.95

BRASS INSTRUMENTS: Their History and Development, Anthony Baines. Authoritative, updated survey of the evolution of trumpets, trombones, bugles, cornets, French horns, tubas and other brass wind instruments. Over 140 illustrations and 48 music examples. Corrected and updated by author. New preface. Bibliography. 320pp. 5⅜ × 8½. 27574-4 Pa. $9.95

HOLLYWOOD GLAMOR PORTRAITS, John Kobal (ed.). 145 photos from 1926-49. Harlow, Gable, Bogart, Bacall; 94 stars in all. Full background on photographers, technical aspects. 160pp. 8⅜ × 11¼. 23352-9 Pa. $11.95

MAX AND MORITZ, Wilhelm Busch. Great humor classic in both German and English. Also 10 other works: "Cat and Mouse," "Plisch and Plumm," etc. 216pp. 5⅜ × 8½. 20181-3 Pa. $5.95

THE RAVEN AND OTHER FAVORITE POEMS, Edgar Allan Poe. Over 40 of the author's most memorable poems: "The Bells," "Ulalume," "Israfel," "To Helen," "The Conqueror Worm," "Eldorado," "Annabel Lee," many more. Alphabetic lists of titles and first lines. 64pp. 5³⁄₁₆ × 8¼. 26685-0 Pa. $1.00

SEVEN SCIENCE FICTION NOVELS, H. G. Wells. The standard collection of the great novels. Complete, unabridged. First Men in the Moon, Island of Dr. Moreau, War of the Worlds, Food of the Gods, Invisible Man, Time Machine, In the Days of the Comet. Total of 1,015pp. 5⅜ × 8½. (USO) 20264-X Clothbd. $29.95

AMULETS AND SUPERSTITIONS, E. A. Wallis Budge. Comprehensive discourse on origin, powers of amulets in many ancient cultures: Arab, Persian, Babylonian, Assyrian, Egyptian, Gnostic, Hebrew, Phoenician, Syriac, etc. Covers cross, swastika, crucifix, seals, rings, stones, etc. 584pp. 5⅜ × 8½. 23573-4 Pa. $12.95

RUSSIAN STORIES/PYCCKNE PACCKA3bl: A Dual-Language Book, edited by Gleb Struve. Twelve tales by such masters as Chekhov, Tolstoy, Dostoevsky, Pushkin, others. Excellent word-for-word English translations on facing pages, plus teaching and study aids, Russian/English vocabulary, biographical/critical introductions, more. 416pp. 5⅜ × 8½. 26244-8 Pa. $8.95

PHILADELPHIA THEN AND NOW: 60 Sites Photographed in the Past and Present, Kenneth Finkel and Susan Oyama. Rare photographs of City Hall, Logan Square, Independence Hall, Betsy Ross House, other landmarks juxtaposed with contemporary views. Captures changing face of historic city. Introduction. Captions. 128pp. 8¼ × 11. 25790-8 Pa. $9.95

AIA ARCHITECTURAL GUIDE TO NASSAU AND SUFFOLK COUNTIES, LONG ISLAND, The American Institute of Architects, Long Island Chapter, and the Society for the Preservation of Long Island Antiquities. Comprehensive, well-researched and generously illustrated volume brings to life over three centuries of Long Island's great architectural heritage. More than 240 photographs with authoritative, extensively detailed captions. 176pp. 8¼ × 11. 26946-9 Pa. $14.95

NORTH AMERICAN INDIAN LIFE: Customs and Traditions of 23 Tribes, Elsie Clews Parsons (ed.). 27 fictionalized essays by noted anthropologists examine religion, customs, government, additional facets of life among the Winnebago, Crow, Zuni, Eskimo, other tribes. 480pp. 6⅛ × 9¼. 27377-6 Pa. $10.95

CATALOG OF DOVER BOOKS

FRANK LLOYD WRIGHT'S HOLLYHOCK HOUSE, Donald Hoffmann. Lavishly illustrated, carefully documented study of one of Wright's most controversial residential designs. Over 120 photographs, floor plans, elevations, etc. Detailed perceptive text by noted Wright scholar. Index. 128pp. 9¼ × 10¾.
27133-1 Pa. $11.95

THE MALE AND FEMALE FIGURE IN MOTION: 60 Classic Photographic Sequences, Eadweard Muybridge. 60 true-action photographs of men and women walking, running, climbing, bending, turning, etc., reproduced from rare 19th-century masterpiece. vi + 121pp. 9 × 12.
24745-7 Pa. $10.95

1001 QUESTIONS ANSWERED ABOUT THE SEASHORE, N. J. Berrill and Jacquelyn Berrill. Queries answered about dolphins, sea snails, sponges, starfish, fishes, shore birds, many others. Covers appearance, breeding, growth, feeding, much more. 305pp. 5¼ × 8¼.
23366-9 Pa. $7.95

GUIDE TO OWL WATCHING IN NORTH AMERICA, Donald S. Heintzelman. Superb guide offers complete data and descriptions of 19 species: barn owl, screech owl, snowy owl, many more. Expert coverage of owl-watching equipment, conservation, migrations and invasions, etc. Guide to observing sites. 84 illustrations. xiii + 193pp. 5⅜ × 8½.
27344-X Pa. $8.95

MEDICINAL AND OTHER USES OF NORTH AMERICAN PLANTS: A Historical Survey with Special Reference to the Eastern Indian Tribes, Charlotte Erichsen-Brown. Chronological historical citations document 500 years of usage of plants, trees, shrubs native to eastern Canada, northeastern U.S. Also complete identifying information. 343 illustrations. 544pp. 6½ × 9¼.
25951-X Pa. $12.95

STORYBOOK MAZES, Dave Phillips. 23 stories and mazes on two-page spreads: Wizard of Oz, Treasure Island, Robin Hood, etc. Solutions. 64pp. 8¼ × 11.
23628-5 Pa. $2.95

NEGRO FOLK MUSIC, U.S.A., Harold Courlander. Noted folklorist's scholarly yet readable analysis of rich and varied musical tradition. Includes authentic versions of over 40 folk songs. Valuable bibliography and discography. xi + 324pp. 5⅜ × 8½.
27350-4 Pa. $7.95

MOVIE-STAR PORTRAITS OF THE FORTIES, John Kobal (ed.). 163 glamor, studio photos of 106 stars of the 1940s: Rita Hayworth, Ava Gardner, Marlon Brando, Clark Gable, many more. 176pp. 8⅜ × 11¼.
23546-7 Pa. $11.95

BENCHLEY LOST AND FOUND, Robert Benchley. Finest humor from early 30s, about pet peeves, child psychologists, post office and others. Mostly unavailable elsewhere. 73 illustrations by Peter Arno and others. 183pp. 5⅜ × 8½.
22410-4 Pa. $5.95

YEKL and THE IMPORTED BRIDEGROOM AND OTHER STORIES OF YIDDISH NEW YORK, Abraham Cahan. Film Hester Street based on Yekl (1896). Novel, other stories among first about Jewish immigrants on N.Y.'s East Side. 240pp. 5⅜ × 8½.
22427-9 Pa. $6.95

SELECTED POEMS, Walt Whitman. Generous sampling from *Leaves of Grass*. Twenty-four poems include "I Hear America Singing," "Song of the Open Road," "I Sing the Body Electric," "When Lilacs Last in the Dooryard Bloom'd," "O Captain! My Captain!"—all reprinted from an authoritative edition. Lists of titles and first lines. 128pp. 5³⁄₁₆ × 8¼.
26878-0 Pa. $1.00

THE BEST TALES OF HOFFMANN, E. T. A. Hoffmann. 10 of Hoffmann's most important stories: "Nutcracker and the King of Mice," "The Golden Flowerpot," etc. 458pp. 5⅜ × 8½. 21793-0 Pa. $8.95

FROM FETISH TO GOD IN ANCIENT EGYPT, E. A. Wallis Budge. Rich detailed survey of Egyptian conception of "God" and gods, magic, cult of animals, Osiris, more. Also, superb English translations of hymns and legends. 240 illustrations. 545pp. 5⅜ × 8½. 25803-3 Pa. $11.95

FRENCH STORIES/CONTES FRANÇAIS: A Dual-Language Book, Wallace Fowlie. Ten stories by French masters, Voltaire to Camus: "Micromegas" by Voltaire; "The Atheist's Mass" by Balzac; "Minuet" by de Maupassant; "The Guest" by Camus, six more. Excellent English translations on facing pages. Also French-English vocabulary list, exercises, more. 352pp. 5⅜ × 8½. 26443-2 Pa. $8.95

CHICAGO AT THE TURN OF THE CENTURY IN PHOTOGRAPHS: 122 Historic Views from the Collections of the Chicago Historical Society, Larry A. Viskochil. Rare large-format prints offer detailed views of City Hall, State Street, the Loop, Hull House, Union Station, many other landmarks, circa 1904–1913. Introduction. Captions. Maps. 144pp. 9⅜ × 12¼. 24656-6 Pa. $12.95

OLD BROOKLYN IN EARLY PHOTOGRAPHS, 1865–1929, William Lee Younger. Luna Park, Gravesend race track, construction of Grand Army Plaza, moving of Hotel Brighton, etc. 157 previously unpublished photographs. 165pp. 8⅞ × 11¾. 23587-4 Pa. $13.95

THE MYTHS OF THE NORTH AMERICAN INDIANS, Lewis Spence. Rich anthology of the myths and legends of the Algonquins, Iroquois, Pawnees and Sioux, prefaced by an extensive historical and ethnological commentary. 36 illustrations. 480pp. 5⅜ × 8½. 25967-6 Pa. $8.95

AN ENCYCLOPEDIA OF BATTLES: Accounts of Over 1,560 Battles from 1479 B.C. to the Present, David Eggenberger. Essential details of every major battle in recorded history from the first battle of Megiddo in 1479 B.C. to Grenada in 1984. List of Battle Maps. New Appendix covering the years 1967–1984. Index. 99 illustrations. 544pp. 6½ × 9¼. 24913-1 Pa. $14.95

SAILING ALONE AROUND THE WORLD, Captain Joshua Slocum. First man to sail around the world, alone, in small boat. One of great feats of seamanship told in delightful manner. 67 illustrations. 294pp. 5⅜ × 8½. 20326-3 Pa. $5.95

ANARCHISM AND OTHER ESSAYS, Emma Goldman. Powerful, penetrating, prophetic essays on direct action, role of minorities, prison reform, puritan hypocrisy, violence, etc. 271pp. 5⅜ × 8½. 22484-8 Pa. $5.95

MYTHS OF THE HINDUS AND BUDDHISTS, Ananda K. Coomaraswamy and Sister Nivedita. Great stories of the epics; deeds of Krishna, Shiva, taken from puranas, Vedas, folk tales; etc. 32 illustrations. 400pp. 5⅜ × 8½. 21759-0 Pa. $9.95

BEYOND PSYCHOLOGY, Otto Rank. Fear of death, desire of immortality, nature of sexuality, social organization, creativity, according to Rankian system. 291pp. 5⅜ × 8½. 20485-5 Pa. $8.95

A THEOLOGICO-POLITICAL TREATISE, Benedict Spinoza. Also contains unfinished Political Treatise. Great classic on religious liberty, theory of government on common consent. R. Elwes translation. Total of 421pp. 5⅜ × 8½. 20249-6 Pa. $8.95

THE INFLUENCE OF SEA POWER UPON HISTORY, 1660–1783, A. T. Mahan. Influential classic of naval history and tactics still used as text in war colleges. First paperback edition. 4 maps. 24 battle plans. 640pp. 5⅜ × 8½.
25509-3 Pa. $12.95

THE STORY OF THE TITANIC AS TOLD BY ITS SURVIVORS, Jack Winocour (ed.). What it was really like. Panic, despair, shocking inefficiency, and a little heroism. More thrilling than any fictional account. 26 illustrations. 320pp. 5⅜ × 8½.
20610-6 Pa. $8.95

FAIRY AND FOLK TALES OF THE IRISH PEASANTRY, William Butler Yeats (ed.). Treasury of 64 tales from the twilight world of Celtic myth and legend: "The Soul Cages," "The Kildare Pooka," "King O'Toole and his Goose," many more. Introduction and Notes by W. B. Yeats. 352pp. 5⅜ × 8½.
26941-8 Pa. $8.95

BUDDHIST MAHAYANA TEXTS, E. B. Cowell and Others (eds.). Superb, accurate translations of basic documents in Mahayana Buddhism, highly important in history of religions. The Buddha-karita of Asvaghosha, Larger Sukhavativyuha, more. 448pp. 5⅜ × 8½. ,
25552-2 Pa. $9.95

ONE TWO THREE . . . INFINITY: Facts and Speculations of Science, George Gamow. Great physicist's fascinating, readable overview of contemporary science: number theory, relativity, fourth dimension, entropy, genes, atomic structure, much more. 128 illustrations. Index. 352pp. 5⅜ × 8½.
25664-2 Pa. $8.95

ENGINEERING IN HISTORY, Richard Shelton Kirby, et al. Broad, nontechnical survey of history's major technological advances: birth of Greek science, industrial revolution, electricity and applied science, 20th-century automation, much more. 181 illustrations. ". . . excellent . . ."—Isis. Bibliography. vii + 530pp. 5⅜ × 8¼.
26412-2 Pa. $14.95